Institutional Br

Exploring mental health nursing practice in acute inpatient settings

Dedications

For my Dad (TF)

For Art O'Driscoll (LC)
1923–1998

Institutional Breakdown:
Exploring mental health nursing practice in acute inpatient settings

by
Liam Clarke
and
Tracy Flanagan

APS Publishing
The Old School, Tollard Royal, Salisbury, Wiltshire, SP5 5PW
www.apspublishing.co.uk

British Library Cataloguing in Publication Data
A catalogue record for this book is available from the British Library

© APS Publishing 2003
ISBN 1 9038771 8 0
Printed in the United Kingdom by Biddles Ltd., Guildford and King's Lynn

Contents

Preface

*T*his book is the product of a series of interviews and sustained observations carried out across five NHS Trusts in South East England during 2000/2001 at the behest of the Trusts concerned. It is a study of how mental health nurses attempt to interact with patients while, at the same time, managing the acute wards to which these patients have been admitted. Throughout, our intention is to provide observation and interview excerpts that represent the most consistently expressed views and concerns of the nurses involved. Rather than adopt an encyclopaedic approach and reproduce responses from each ward, we chose, instead, to identify those concerns that were typical of all of the wards, omitting material that seemed peculiar to any one unit. This did result in a loss of some challenging and interesting material, but we needed to represent views fairly and comprehensively.

It was decided to abbreviate the final Report in the interests of accessibility (and readability) but, at the same time, to retain a formal approach and structure in setting out our findings. To that end, a series of formal recommendations are attached at the end of *Chapter 9*, recommendations that we believe are justified in the light of our discoveries. We hope that you will agree.

Chapter 1
Introduction:
The recurring problem

*T*his project arose from local acknowledgement of nation-
ally identified problems within acute psychiatric adult inpatient settings. A raft of recent reports had highlighted a
lack of therapeutic culture and activity in these settings, together with patient dissatisfaction and a chronic failure to address research developments in practice (Baker, 2000;
Sainsbury, 1998; Simpson, 1998; SNMAC, 1999). All these Reports suggested a need for movement towards an evidence-based culture within these settings. In particular, it was
felt that nurses ought to be better placed to account for their
work with patients in ways that are manifestly measurable
and accountable.

Locally, a bid was made by the Sussex Education Consortium (SEC, 1999) to commission a project that would focus on
professional practice within the five trusts providing mental
health services in their area. It was suggested that the design
of the project should allow for the 'examination of evidence-
based practice in acute, adult psychiatric inpatient units for
people suffering with psychotic illness.' To that end, 200 hours
of observations were carried out by one of the researchers
within the acute inpatient settings of the five trusts involved,
coupled with a series of interviews involving 52 qualified
nurses, an examination of 32 sets of nursing notes and various
other documentation.

First steps

Initially, a series of investigations/outcomes were prescribed so that a baseline of current services could be established. These involved:

- Benchmarking current practice across the five trusts providing acute inpatient care
- Focussing on practice within the acute assessment areas
- Focussing on patients suffering with a psychotic illness
- Reviewing policy/documentation to determine what should happen, what nurses say happens and what nurses actually do
- Looking at from where nurses get their evidence base and what they want in terms of training and development.

In addition, a project steering group comprised of representatives from the respective trusts was set up to oversee the general progress of the study and to act as a consultant group in respect of difficulties overlooked, or other complex problems.

The context

Concerns regarding the state of inpatient acute psychiatric settings had been gathering momentum for years. Peplau (1994) feared that nursing within these settings was in danger of returning to the custodialism of the nineteenth century, with an increasing marginalisation of nurturing and a return to predominantly medical-led interventions. Dennis (1997) argued that a growing authoritarianism in community psychiatric care was being reflected in inpatient settings, with increasing numbers of locked admission wards echoing the situation at the turn of the century when all psychiatric doors were locked. Gournay *et al* (1998) catalogued the progression of psychiatric nursing through the last half of the century and concluded that, despite several philosophical and practice developments, custodial care had again become the norm in inpatient settings.

Cleary and Edwards (1999) argued that this return to custodial, non-therapeutic approaches was about nurses trying to adapt to the increasing pressures of acute inpatient services, such as staff shortages, plus the ever increasing necessity to accommodate troublesome patients, perhaps brutalised by the discriminatory effects of a community care system shorn of adequate facilities. The Standing Nursing and Midwifery Advisory Committee (SNMAC, 1999) Report, 'Addressing Acute Concerns', identified a decrease in the number of acute beds in recent years such that those inhabiting the beds were now much more likely to have psychotic illnesses, possess a dual diagnosis, or other complex social problems. Parallel with these developments was an increase in the number of patients being compulsorily admitted under the Mental Health Act (Baker, 2000). Although the last 20 years had seen a rapid growth in the provision of forensic facilities for disordered offenders (Butler, 1974), this had not lessened—it may even have contributed to—the emergent custodial mentality of the millennium period.

'Addressing Acute Concerns' (SNMAC, 1999) highlighted a lack of clinical leadership in mainstream acute psychiatric settings, compounded by shifts in emphasis in education, training, status, and career opportunities from inpatient to community settings and other specialist areas. Whatever deficiencies community provision might possess, it nevertheless attracted more attention than inpatient services, and community psychiatric nurses (CPNs) seemed to enjoy more varied and autonomous career pathways. An interesting aside is that, although CPNs are dwarfed in number by inpatient nurses, the former, unlike the latter, have their own journal, their own annual conference and a disproportional voice in professional discussion and debate. 'Addressing Acute Concerns' also noted the paucity of research into inpatient nursing care, resulting in a deficient knowledge base, which in turn aggravated recurring—and to some extent induced—problems within inpatient settings.

'Acute Problems' (Sainsbury, 1998) argued that many admissions to inpatient services could be avoided, but that community services were failing to predict or prevent these admissions. It also showed that patients were subsequently not being discharged from hospital because of inadequate community resources. This inevitably impacted on the quality of the experiences of patients who were now occupying hospital beds much longer than necessary. The Report also highlighted an absence of full multidisciplinary and community team involvement in inpatient care: the standard picture seemed to be that, once admitted, the main input to patient care and treatment came from insular teams of ward-based nurses and doctors.

Both Reports ('Acute Problems' and 'Addressing Acute Concerns') concluded that staffing levels and skill mix were so poor that ward environments were inadequate, even for the provision of basic safety and patient comfort. Added to which, they were also seen as lacking the basic resources required to formulate a therapeutic culture and thus make positive clinical interventions feasible.

Further evidence of the inadequacy of inpatient environments was provided by the MIND Report 'Environmentally Friendly' (Baker, 2000), which solicited information from psychiatric service users through postal questionnaires. More than half of these respondents stated that they had not found inpatient environments therapeutic, with many describing the atmosphere as depressing; indeed, for most of them, the final outcome of their inpatient stay was a negative effect on their mental health. From the perspective of nursing staff, 'Addressing Acute Concerns' (SNMAC, 1999) described working in these environments as a demoralising experience, with nurses bereft of decent clinical leadership, adequate education, training, or support. The levels of stress experienced by nurses were described as unacceptably high and, predictably, this produced stressful consequences, such as increased sickness levels, absenteeism, and interpersonal conflict.

Damning

These various reports present a fairly damning indictment of inpatient services and an extensive review of the wider literature found little positive contrast. Yet as Moore (1998) pointed out, inpatient services persist as a key component within mental health provision and absorb a large chunk of the financial allocation for psychiatric care: according to Ford (2002) this amounts to 25% of the mental health budget (about £800m per annum). While the psychiatric hospitals have now closed, provision for the admission and treatment of acutely ill psychiatric patients proceeds apace under various guises. In the geographic region covered by this study, all the acute wards previously housed within the old mental hospitals continue either as purpose built units in the grounds of district general hospitals, or in newly created satellite units. The oft-heard cry 'they shouldn't have closed the mental hospitals' is a hollow protest: the hospitals really did not close at all. The physical buildings that housed them closed: many of their central functions, however, were simply transferred and this seems to have been overlooked or forgotten. Even when the number of hospital beds had dramatically dropped, the number of admissions increased—from 156,000 in 1965 to 199,000 in 1985—due to people having sequences of admissions and discharges instead of the older pattern of hospital admission for extended periods of time (or for life).

The hospital closures did not bring about sufficient compensatory community-centred services adequate to meet the needs of discharged patients; the inpatient services that remained have thus continued to experience difficulties in ensuring good practice and acceptable standards for their patients. We have ended up with the worst of both worlds: the continued institutionalisation of psychotic and personality disordered patients in hospital settings, many of which have become isolated—literally and metaphorically—from contemporary thinking about psychiatric practice. In particular, modern-day nurse education institutes, ensconced in the new universities, are effectively cut adrift from where patient care is actually delivered. In addition, their obsession with theory has diminished their capacity to influence or improve practice.

Perhaps the most peculiar feature of acute inpatient settings is their over-population by patients with very varied mental disorders, so that, from a nursing perspective, a coherent therapeutic strategy becomes implausible; the situation quickly becomes one of mere management and containment.

Community implications

The community psychiatric nurses have had to come to (grudging) terms with an inpatient capacity of relentless insufficiency; this is especially true in respect of psychotic and aggressive patients. Since the inception of community psychiatric nursing (within the region covered by this study), its concerns have diverged, mainly between care for the elderly, coupled with a growing involvement with counselling patients perhaps less seriously ill than others. Partly as a result of the growing inability of inpatient settings to cope effectively with psychotic patients, CPNs have had to alter their role to take account of such patients for whom hospital beds have now become scarce. Part of that 'taking account', however, has paradoxically resulted in an increased pressure on the acute wards to take such patients and the burden on these wards has not decreased.

For many the situation is unacceptable and needs to be addressed. The problem, as Baker (2000) points out, is that 'reviews of poor practice and deficient standards are important, but do not indicate future direction.' In fact, these reports have spawned a plethora of recommendations along with, in the literature, much debate and informal prescription about what should or could be done. The responsibility for action and change usually ranges from the political and legislative at national and local level to individual nursing responses within practice areas. Neither the collective nor the individual political will can work successfully without the other, however, and any proposals for change will have to embrace factors pitched both at micro and macro levels.

Evidenced-based practice

One theme that has dominated all of the various reports and recent discussion is the question of 'evidence-based practice'. The policy framework for increasing the emphasis on evidence-based practice and the accountability of practitioners was set out in the Government white paper, 'The New NHS' (Department of Health, 1997). The subsequent publication of 'Modernising Mental Health Services' (Department of Health, 1998) and the National Service Framework for Mental Health (Department of Health, 1999a) set the agenda for priorities, standards and outcomes that would comprise a defined evidence base. These reports also made clear that the development of interventions based on evidence was only a first step and that a strategy for the dissemination of best practice was also required.

While many of these reports, for example 'Acute Problems' (Sainsbury, 1998), 'Addressing Acute Concerns' (SNMAC, 1999) and 'Environmentally Friendly' (Baker, 2000) have recommended an improved evidence base in psychiatric nursing practice and while all of them posited that training, education and research were needed in support of this, their rhetoric failed to say how such practice would translate into actual service provision.

One major problem is that, despite the overarching responsibility of providers to ensure that evidence-based practice is integrated into service provision (as well as their apparent keenness to do so), the implementation of such practice lies with practitioners. As Miller and Crabtree (2000: 613) observe: 'Local politics and contradictory demands become hushed as does the effects on evidence-based practice of individual clinical expertise and the associated areas of relationship dynamics, communication, and patient preference; there is much to be learned about how patients and clinicians actually implement best evidence'. This problem has led to confusion in terms of determining where responsibility for implementing and managing evidence-based practice should lie. One report by the English National Board (ENB, 2000) 'Team

Working in Mental Health', suggested that research-based approaches were needed most at policy development levels. For example, several writers have identified policy issues of relevance to acute inpatient services, such as admission criteria, alternatives to admission, multi-disciplinary team working, risk management, and resource allocation (Croudace *et al*, 1998; Bartlett *et al*, 1999; Baker, 2000). However, while it might be relatively easy to generate empirical, replicable data in respect of these organisational aspects of care, it might prove more difficult to construct an evidence base that can be applied satisfactorily across the wide range of ways in which nurses interact with their patients. Herein lies the crux of the matter: for, as we shall see, many nurses in this study espoused a broad-based humanistic (or Rogerian) stance—a stance that could be said to have dominated British psychiatric nursing over the last 30 years—but possessing an 'evidence' base that is hardly amenable to measurement or evaluation.

Alternatively, some implicitly accepted frameworks (such as cognitive behaviour therapy), which did lend themselves to the types of evidence base set out by the various commissioned reports; and some evinced no framework at all other than a 'natural affinity' with medical practice or a basic orientation rooted in intuition and experience. As Wilson and Kneisl (1988) point out, to assert, as many do, that nurses base their practices on abstract philosophies is 'probably naive: treatment ideologies and practices are intertwined with the everyday realities of the work situation. In her groundbreaking study, 'Patient Nurse Interaction', Altschul (1972) suggested that nurses did not possess any identifiable perspective to guide them in their dealings with problematic issues. As a generalisation, this hardly holds true any longer but, as evidenced in this study, a worryingly large number of nurses still perform their role without reference to any standard criteria or theory. A minority of nurses, mainly those working within nurse educational establishments, are worried about this and it is that worry, allied to governmental and administrative anxieties about NHS productivity and outcomes, which has produced demands for evidence-based (accountable) practice.

The emphasis is on quantitative measurement, accountability, the desire to obtain value for money, and the rooting out of ineffectiveness.

We feel that the imperative to develop and implement evidence-based procedures requires a description of, and consensus about, what counts as evidence and to whom. To some extent a 'rhetoric of evidence' has gained credence (and kudos) because it taps into a political ideology of value for money in the NHS, and the demand that professionals supply proof that what they do is worthwhile.

The various reports cited here assume that the nature of the evidence base is a 'given' and with a further built-in assumption that nursing will, as in the past, uncritically accept major proposals affecting its practice. The maturity of a profession, however, is its ability and willingness to doubt and discuss its concerns. We would like to inquire, therefore, whether or not the quality of relationships between psychiatric nurses and patients is measurable. Although specific psychological therapies may generate tangible outcomes, are such outcomes feasible when what is at stake are, for example, levels of mutual respect and regard, or the maintenance of someone's dignity or self-esteem? We think it worthwhile, as a starting point, to examine the nature of evidence and its relevance to the care of patients.

Chapter 2
The nature of evidence

*T*his is a complex and emotive area encompassing as it does practical and philosophical issues. Recourse to the literature provides a rich, but confusing picture mainly because the term 'evidence' has different meanings depending on who uses the term and for what purpose. However, it can be asserted that the current preoccupation with evidence-based practice, by nurses, has proceeded without due attention to the philosophical issues involved, so that what is normally counted as evidence is tangible data susceptible to quantifiable measurement and replication, ideally using randomised control trials (RCTs). According to Goding and Edwards (2002: 46)

> *'These trials are usually intended to generate quantitative data and are said to minimise the operation of bias and chance findings. Qualitative non-controlled studies are sometimes criticised as being too subjective and more difficult to interpret'.*

The National Service Framework (Department of Health, 1999a) provides a hierarchy of evidence types:

- **Type 1 evidence**—At least one good systematic review, including at least one RCT
- **Type 2 evidence**—At least one good RCT
- **Type 3 evidence**—At least one well designed intervention study, but without randomisation
- **Type 4 evidence**—At least one well designed observational study
- **Type 5 evidence**—Expert opinion, including the opinion of service users and carers: in other words, qualitative research.

A frequently cited problem is the paucity of Type 1 and 2 evidence relating to mental health nursing generally and, more specifically, to mental health nursing in inpatient settings

(Parahoo, 1999). When Jones *et al* (2000) reviewed the Cochrane Library (an Internet and CD-ROM facility developed internationally to provide for the dissemination of 'the best available external clinical evidence from systematic research') they identified only four psychiatric nursing studies, which fulfilled the criteria for Type 1 and Type 2 evidence. In Parahoo's (1999) view, while psychiatric nursing research was on the increase, it was still focussed on exploring and describing the processes and contexts of care and not the measurement of outcomes. A particular difficulty in executing nursing research is that quantifying process is difficult, since many of the variables inherent in patients' lifestyles and daily living are outside experimental control. Arguably, this limits the use of RCTs other than for investigations of specific physical treatments or therapeutic interventions that do not consider the socio-economic, domestic and personal contexts of patients' lives.

Sullivan (1998) acknowledges the limitations of RCTs precisely because of their failure to account for human complexity. However, he also criticises the subjectivity of qualitative designs, concluding that many of these are weak both in design and methodology. Cutcliffe (1997) states that qualitative approaches are more relevant to psychiatric nursing due to a 'synchronicity' between them and important aspects of nurse-patient interactions. These include the therapeutic use of self, the ability to embrace ambiguity, uncertainty and even rejection. The central difficulty seems to be to provide research strategies that take account of human subjectivity and diversity without, at the same time, sacrificing methodological rigour.

Gordon (1998) linked the limited amount of psychiatric nursing research to an identity crisis fostered by dependence on medical concerns. Further uncertainty is generated by the divergent views held by influential nursing academics relating to the causes and treatment of mental illness and the relevant implications for psychiatric nursing. For example, Gournay (1996) has advocated a quasi medical role for nurses comprised of nurse prescribing, attention to the physical causes of psychiatric illness, and the adoption of cognitive behaviourism. Barker (2000), alternatively challenges psychiatric nurses to risk more passive engagements with patients, ones that respect experience as the ultimate arbiter of well-being and recovery. While such disagreements about the nature of psychiatric illness and nursing may delay the development of a viable knowledge base, others (Cutcliffe, 1997; Chambers, 1998) see this ongoing polarisation as a reflection of academic maturity. The latter is probably true enough; the problem is that, while this internecine strife engages the minds of a minority of theoretical activists, the large majority of practitioners probably do not connect with it. Although practitioners pay scant attention to academic debate, if such debate was capable of evolving a coherent model or strategy, then to some extent, this might alleviate the uncertainty surrounding practice in general.

Research and practice

The translation of research into practice is fraught with difficulties (Kitson *et al*, 1996; Tarrier *et al*, 1999; Richardson and Droogan, 1999). From time immemorial, nursing has weathered stormy disputes concerning its 'theory practice divide': a strong lobby has always regarded nursing as a practical undertaking possessed of a service (vocational) ethic and obligated to the basic needs of patients; this lobby has traditionally been content to take the direction of physicians on questions of treatments. In general, it favours training rather than education and research is given a low priority: for a summary of this position set within recent historical nursing developments, see Bradshaw (2001).

The academic and professionaliser's view, however, is that nursing is a 'proper' profession that must develop its knowledge base independently of medicine; the nurse is an autonomous practitioner who makes decisions about patients' health and well-being and, to do this successfully, she needs a body of evidence upon which to base her interventions. These 'professionalisers' inhabit the academic citadels of nurse education now located inside the newer universities. A small number also inhabit practice areas mainly in management or 'nurse consultant' roles. Of course, over the last twenty years or so, there has occurred a meeting of the ways and some 'shop-floor' practitioners now acknowledge that research—particularly when emerging from practice settings—can have value. Similarly, academics have had to temper their idealism and in a post Project 2000 world—over the last three years or so—the harsh practicalities of ward-based requirements have begun to make themselves felt, and educational programmes have become more realistic.

In general, nurses' attitudes towards research also vary in relation to their position within health care organisations: health service managers, for example, often concentrate on short-term training projects aimed at addressing specific clinical outcomes and, as a rule, are reluctant to support in depth or long-term courses. Nurses do not, as such, necessarily inhabit research orientated work settings: their organisations may have other agendas and, in any event, the sheer press of clinical work often militates against reflection and inquiry. Unsurprisingly, work can become repetitive and progressively grounded in ritual and routine. Tordoff (1998) supports the view that cultural, organisational and personal factors constrain nursing research and, undoubtedly, organisational and administrative factors remain important barriers to furthering nursing investigations.

Psychiatric nursing *per se?*

An initial assumption might be that psychiatric nursing is quintessentially a social engagement that transcends (but can include) therapeutic involvement. Chambers (1998) states:

> *'To distil the nature of mental health nursing knowledge and its associated clinical practice, research activity should be grounded largely in an understanding of what it means to be human' (p204).*

Illingworth (1999) asserts that psychiatric nursing is about caring and compassion and that the 'evidence' needing to be utilised in education, research, practice, and service development involves understanding of patients' opinions and perceptions. This is supported by Perkins (2000) who maintains that people with mental health problems develop an individual expertise, an 'evidence base' of their own experiences. Presumably, to exclude this experience would be detrimental to patient care. Godfrey and Wistow (1997) describe patients' views of therapeutic effectiveness as based not only on a reduction of their symptoms, but also on relationships with professionals that inculcate understanding, respect and dignity, as well as a recognition (by patients) of how their illness impacts on the broader aspects of their lives.

Crook (2001) cited the importance of 'knowing patients' in the process of selecting appropriate ways of working with them. Benner (1984) gives examples of what she calls 'expert nursing' that does not rely on assessment processes to determine a course of action, but on the nurse's instinctive knowledge of what the patient experiences. The implication is that expertise and knowledge derived from practice cannot be 'squeezed' into a positivistic framework because positivism leads to strategies, which particularise patient's problems in ways that make them susceptible to specific treatments. Crook's (2001) view and Benner's (1984) is that expertise (in nursing) is a process that operates from a deep understanding of the whole situation, this being construed as an intermingling of patients' symptoms plus patients' own perceptions of these, their social and psychological implications and, of course, the value systems and beliefs of involved professionals.

One could, of course, equally see Benner and Crooks' holism as reflecting the difficulties involved in describing specific nursing expertise in treatment settings. It has been suggested that nurses should strive to employ specific therapeutic strategies, such as those based on cognitive-behaviourism, and abandon holistic-based concepts, such as those advocated by Benner. However, the view that nursing is about caring for individuals in defined settings and not exclusively a treatment modality has perhaps won more support. Schon (1983: 46) expresses this rather well, stating that 'convergent knowledge, derived from rigorous research methodologies, fails to resolve practice situations that are uncertain, unique and unstable'. He describes processes of 'reflection in action' whereby professionals respond instinctively to the situations they encounter. According to Schon, this 'art' is difficult to teach, but it can be nurtured by valuing the knowledge that individuals acquire and possess through experience, experience that cannot always be articulated, quantified, or measured. Clearly, in terms of evolving an evidence base, there are going to be difficulties in this area. How can we be sure, and what level of intimacy would be required, to know that patients were not telling us simply what they wanted us to hear? Or, from a psychoanalytic viewpoint, what credibility would we accord to patients' manifest statements as opposed to beliefs about their unconscious meaning?

Low priority

The low premium placed on intangible forms of evidence [in the National Service Framework (Department of Health, 1999a) for example] has caused consternation among some observers (Perkins, 2000; Illingworth, 1999): but, as we have seen, evidence-based practice is typically seen as conceptually linked to empirical (in the sense of quantitative) research with the kinds of variables listed by Schon being seen as somehow second rate, anecdotal, and 'soft'. In our view, a narrow empiricism such as this would probably limit both the range and depth of much nursing research. While allowing that important differences exist between quantitative and qualitative studies, psychiatric care ought to be open to forms of inquiry whose evidence base incorporates experiential as well as (or even instead of) quantitative data.

The point being that what counts as evidence depends on the kinds of questions for which answers are being sought, the contexts or situations in which these questions—perhaps necessarily—occur, and the overall purpose to which investigations are directed. In judicial settings, for example, the subjectivity of witnesses constantly comes up against the quest for precision and nowhere is this laid more bare than when unfortunate juries must interpret the biassed summaries put to them by duelling lawyers—and a not always impartial judge. The process can hardly be called scientific: even the rigour of judicial rules governing evidence hardly counteracts the preconceived notions of jury members. It is a sobering thought that, if a jury was substituted or even part substituted with other jurors, alternative verdicts might well occur. It is always possible that the more tangible and explicit the evidence presented, the less likely it is that this might happen: but judicious processes are imperfect as frequent instances of rough and miscarried justice shows. The same set of problems beset qualitative researchers: just like the lawyers, they too are asking their audiences to take—as a matter of trust—subjective findings and interpretations acquired through observations and interviews. Why should they be believed?

We believe that such criticisms carry some weight. However, it is also the case that, in psychiatric nursing, subjective style investigations are necessary and, given the particular nature of many nursing problems, might be the only approaches capable of yielding meaningful results that would make sense of nursing as a social (interpersonal) and organisational enterprise. Discussing the value of everyday terms as explanatory mechanisms (in addition to scientific terms) Mary Midgley (2001: 11) states that, 'Words such as *care, heart, spirit, sense,* [her italics] are tools designed for particular kinds of work in the give-and-take of social life. They are not a cheap substitute, an inadequate folk psychology, due to be replaced by the proper terms of the learned'.

Further, in connection with some nursing questions—the experience of pain for example—we submit that more scientific methods might be counterproductive, might detract from an area of inquiry where the testimony (of sufferers) is sacrosanct. When Midgley goes on to say that such words come from 'underlying world visions', which imbue both science and poetry such that any faults they may have are reflecting those visions, the point can be applied to the nature of evidence, the interpretation of which is also at the mercy of pre-existing world views. All argument, said Nietzsche, reflects a desire of the heart and we can be relatively certain that 'the evidence' may be understood in a variety of ways.

An alternative view

Kitson (1997) points out that confusion attends the terms 'evidence-based medicine' and 'clinical effectiveness': this is true inasmuch as the evidence that a procedure is effective is not evidence that the principles upon which the intervention is based are true: the two do not follow. Indeed, clinical effectiveness can proceed even in the absence of any evidence as to why: it is still uncertain why the electrical treatment of depression works; however, the 'evidence of our eyes'—patient improvement following the use of this treatment—suggests that it does. The potential contradictions between theory and efficacy is probably best seen between the two psychological schools, behaviourism and psychoanalysis where, arguably, psychoanalysis has exercised a disproportionate influence on intellectual thought, but is nowadays seen as having only modest utility as a therapy. Behaviourism, alternatively, can seem limited when attempting to explain human affairs, but it has achieved significant therapeutic effectiveness. For Stevens (1976: 33) 'psychoanalytic treatment is perhaps best regarded not as a therapy, but as an intensive form of education in self-awareness. Definitive behavioural changes will not *necessarily* (his italics) be expected as a result of this.' This is probably true of a whole range of psychotherapies where 'outcomes' are going to be vague and difficult to describe in evidence-based terms. And while effectiveness is not necessarily dependant on the truth or otherwise of underlying principles, this point is probably going to be lost on health service managers or other agencies who fund research studies.

An additional problem is that evidence is only useful therapeutically where nurses have control over their interventions with patients. As this study will show, in hospital-based settings such control is still far from being the norm. Yet few would deny that nurses exert positive and negative effects on the outcomes of their patient's illnesses as well as their general welfare. The question is whether this stems from a generalised application of compassion coupled with a measure of medical skills, or if it results from autonomous professionalism derived from an evidence base and informed by scientific principles. If the latter, then what is the nature of that evidence? The aforementioned small number of nursing studies included in the Cochrane Library suggests that nursing has yet to establish itself as an evidence-based profession. And it is quite startling that, although nursing has not yet provided an adequate description of what it is, some nurses seek to embrace evidence-based practice. Advocates of such practice, for instance Kitson (1997: 38), recognise that the rules governing evidenced-based practice are:

> 'about medical diagnosis, single clinical interventions, RCTs and meta analyses. It is acknowledged that there is a limit to nursing evidence conforming to these criteria.'

But even if such evidence is acquired, is it nursing evidence? Or is it medical evidence acquired by people employed as nurses in a secondary role to medics? If not a secondary (but instead equal) role, then if the evidence being collected is medical in nature, why not abolish nursing altogether? Or relegate its non (strictly) medical functions to another group?

Overweening belief

Professor Gail Stuart is an advocate of evidence-based psychiatric nursing. She states (2001: 103) that psychiatric nursing 'can no longer rely on opinion-based processes or unproven theories', but must opt instead for an evidenced-based practice that can 'have a transformative effect on the specialty.' By evidence-based practice, she means the explicit use of 'best evidence' derived from systematic research. The key phrase here is *systematic* because it signifies that the best evidence—the only evidence—comes from studies that isolate and control variables so as to produce findings, which can be replicated. Such studies are made easier when they can be quantified, their hypotheses and investigative methods set out in numerical terms. The kinds of tests best embodying these ambitions are randomised control trials (RCTs) and these have undoubtedly stood the test of time in medical and pharmacological research. Professor Stuart (2001: 104) is not shy in advocating these sorts of studies:

> *'The best basis to substantiate clinical practice is the evidence of well-established clinical findings. Such evidence reflects verifiable, replicable facts and relationships that have been exposed to stringent scientific criteria. This research has less potential for bias than the other bases for practice, most particularly the traditional 'that's how we've always done it' basis for practice.'*

The comparison between scientific method and nursing ritual is perhaps a shade absolute here, although plainly the distinction being made is also between scientific rigour and 'the other bases for practice'. This dismissal needs to be examined to see if it stands up. Before doing so, a perusal of how Professor Stuart develops her views about evidence will prove instructive since her views are not untypical of evidence-based advocates generally. She begins by acknowledging that 'not all clinical practice can or should be based on science' and lists the following exclusions: issues involving ethics, patient situations that are 'very complex', and situations where clinical acumen is important. In other words, having ruled out clinical practice derived from tradition, she then allows that 'judgement[s] developed from experience [are] essential to psychiatric nursing practice' (p104). In the present context, Cullum (1997) states that:

> *'Nursing, along with the other healthcare professions must seek to establish the effectiveness of its practices. Nurses choices should be informed by evidence ' (p4).*

Cullum then bemoans the comparative absence of RCTs in the nursing literature. Nurses, it seems, favour qualitative designs and, in this instance, she says that:

> *'there is something of an 'antitrial' culture in nursing in the United Kingdom, where nurses seem particularly keen to adopt research designs which are clearly different from their medical colleagues. Thus, papers which argue for qualitative research in preference to the quantitative—for example RCTs—abound'* (p5).

Analysing evidence

Actually, the drive in nursing is not so much fuelled by an antitrial culture as much as it is for independent status as a profession. Adult nurses—or elitist groups within adult nursing—have fought to establish for themselves a theory or knowledge base that would give nursing autonomous professional status (Humphreys, 1996; Bradshaw, 2001). To that end, they sought to distance nursing from any notions of handmaiden ideology by constructing alternative frameworks for its discourse and 'knowledge base'. The adoption of holistic philosophy with its emphasis on person-centredness partly accounts for the emphasis on qualitative studies. These are seen as more intuitively sensitive to the kinds of 'whole' person philosophising espoused by nurses. Of course, the realities of working in medical-surgical settings, as well as the basic orientations of most practising nurses continued much as before, one upshot of this discrepancy being the rekindling of a more virulent theory/practice gap. And it is this gap that remains relatively unexplored, especially within inpatient settings. As this study shows, nursing practice can often proceed without any reflective thought whatsoever. This appears to be because the conditions of care delivery are simply not conducive to reflection and where patients are simply made as medically fit as possible in the limited time allowed.

It is important, therefore, to tease apart different groups of nurses and their attendant beliefs. It was adult, not psychiatric, nurses who vociferously championed a new and independent role; their influence mirrored their predominance among influential (London-based) organisations, such as the Royal College of Nursing and the Department of Health. Historically, their identity had been enmeshed with the medical profession and this was the link that they wanted to sever. Although psychiatric nurses were similarly entwined with medical psychiatry, psychiatry itself sported a chequered past in terms of establishing an identity as a medical speciality. From within psychiatry's ranks, sceptical minorities had always questioned the validity of its medical claims (Szasz, 1974; Bracken and Thomas, 1999), to which can be added a number of like-minded psychiatric nurses (Barker, 2000; Rolfe, 2000). The important distinction between psychiatric nurses and their adult colleagues (in this context) is that psychiatric nurses are less concerned about ascending professional peaks, being more eager to critique the scientific pretensions of psychiatric medicine.

Evidently, beliefs about the nature of psychological disturbance are going to produce different kinds of investigator-involvement with patients than, say, questions about pressure sores. Cullum (1997) is concerned that nursing still lacks 'a scientific basis for the prevention of pressure sores'. This is surprising and one wonders why. Surely, there are medical rationales for dealing with pressure sores; why can't nurses utilise one of these? What would constitute a *'nursing* scientific' basis for dealing with pressure sores and how would it differ from a medical approach? Of course, the answer is that it wouldn't and that what these nurse scientists fail to identify are the non-medical features of nursing, which sets it apart from other professions. On the question of pressure sores, what is important is their prevention, particularly in the elderly. In effect, where the medical 'condition' has yet to come into existence, the basic skills of nursing can be applied with good preventative results. This is not enough for some, though, and the move (from nursing) into treatment has proved an irresistible as well as necessary professional move.

Our purpose at this point is not to score points, but to highlight some difficulties that campaigners for evidence-based practice—empirical, quantitative, replicable evidence—will face and especially since the nature of nursing care, particularly psychiatric nursing care, is not yet established. For example, can there be any area of psychiatric care that does not involve ethical or experiential dimensions? If judgements stemming from professional experience are important (and they are), should they take precedence over the evidence if so warranted by individual or social need? If, for example, 'the evidence' suggests a course of action for a particular patient, how does the patient's refusal to accept it—for example, medication—affect the evidence? If, from an ethical perspective, I regard the patient's refusal as valid, what do I then do with evidence that points to 'non-compliance' as a symptom of illness? Do I set this symptomology aside in favour of the patient's view? For it is this 'setting aside' of the patient's view—his humanity—which has been a cornerstone of institutional nursing and which now finds expression in an increasingly custodial-minded community care (Radcliffe, 2002). In their study, 'Relative Values', Shepherd *et al* (1994: 53) found sharp differences between users and carers on the issue of self-determination:

> *'There was a strong feeling from family carers concerning the scope of the current Mental Health Act, whose safeguards for the individual rights of the user were perceived to run contrary to their needs for care, especially where the person was at risk of self-neglect.'*

Differences of priority between professionals and patients are even more accentuated when, in the case of hospitalised patients, their rights (even, occasionally, against the best efforts of nurses) are run roughshod over by institutional demands and economic shortages. Currently, there is much evidence—in the form of widespread dissension by professional organisations—against the imposition of the Government's new mental health act, but it seems unlikely that this dissension will be given much heed (Radcliffe 2002). Clearly, the uses to which evidence is put is important and what might seem to be crucial to one group might not seem so to another. Evidence serves purposes and we have tried to show how, in the case of adult nurses, a rhetoric of evidence and 'knowledge base' was used to bolster professional claims. Equally, upon what evidence is the proposed mental health legislation based? Given that all the relevant professional bodies have protested its inception, is the evidence which supports it based purely on political fear? Nothing wrong with that, but it does raise questions about what counts as evidence.

What is evidence?

Stuart (2001: 104) says that defining terms is crucial:

'The formulation of a precise clinical question involves defining the patient's problems…and specifying the expected outcomes.'

This should be done, she says, in partnership with the patient. The next step is to find the evidence and this, she says, takes the form of exhaustive examinations of published studies— preferably RCTs—so as to find the best treatment. Bearing in mind that Stuart is writing within a nursing context, the emphasis on treatment seems initially confusing. The emphatic shift from a patient who, minutes earlier, the nurse was working in partnership with (so as to elucidate his or her problems) is passed by. Evidence, in this context, is not the patient's perceptions of relationships with others: personal experience has been put on the back burner. Of course, this is acceptable if trying to determine the best drug for an illness or even when working out what psychological intervention to use: for example, obsessive compulsive disorder is ideally treated using cognitive-behaviourist techniques. Herein lies a problem: if nurses are effective, is it because they are therapists whose treatment modalities operate independently of relationships or, is nursing something that is distilled through pathways from ethical to political to spiritual; if the latter, what is the evidence base for these? This is not to say that therapy cannot encompass emotion: as well as dealing with pressure sores, the therapist (be it doctor or nurse) also has regard for the affected individual, but the essence of what is done (in evidence-based terms) is medical by nature: the 'regard' which they display for the patient is evidence of their humanitarianism, but it does not lend itself to proof and you cannot teach it; neither can it be operationalised as an outcome or product.

In his paper, 'The Nonsense of Effectiveness', Don Bannister (1998 reprint) asserts that in much of what passes for psychotherapy, the 'medical model' still governs our thinking. If we substituted any common term for 'psychotherapy' such as 'conversation', then, he says:

'if you were asked how effective is conversation, you would surely begin by questioning the question. As it stands it is nonsense' (p218).

And yet, we are continuously asked for evidence that our conversations with patients are effective: the assumption seems to be that all listening and talking must possess a formal base. The issue is not one of 'either/or', of desiring to segregate scientific inquiries into matters to do with neurones and galvanic responses; it is conceded that there are psychological interventions that can be quantitatively measured and this is true for some social interactions as well. But it is not true for all, no more than it is for some of the most important interactions which influence how people deal with their illnesses and problems.

Advocates of evidence-based approaches make heavy weather of the need to prove effectiveness: according to Professor Stuart (2001), psychiatric nurses need to describe what they do 'with sensitivity to the issues of effectiveness' (p109). However, effectiveness evidence is usually found within the (learned) journal claims of medical and allied practice, as well as behaviourally directed psychologies. Rather than inquire about how psychiatric nursing might differ from these schools, it is simply assumed that psychiatric nurses who lack this evidence of effectiveness must be somehow deficient. To return to Bannister:

'Are you really prepared to contend that your relationships, your love affairs, your enmities, your long standing dialogue with your uncle Albert—whether the effect be good, bad or chaotic—have been, in some strange sense, ineffective?' (p219).

Admittedly, personal relationships do not constitute psychotherapy. If one sets out to help people's psychological problems, there occurs some obligation to adopt professional techniques, some acknowledgment, as well, that one can alleviate the problems. That said, many nurses engage with patients in ways that do resemble loving relationships and, arguably, psychotherapy is about harnessing the trust, mutual respect, and acceptance (or otherwise) which exists in these relationships in the service of helping the patient.

In Bannister's view, proving effectiveness—especially when the financial costs of therapy are an issue—constitutes a moral imperative that needs to be resisted. To pay attention to an individual (which is the essence of most psychotherapy) is also to commit a moral act. In essence, it respects the patient's experience of the world. Cost is always a factor to be considered, but cost can be used to blackmail nurses whose orientation is about respecting patients' views and creating time and space for them to express them. To some extent, differences in orientation reflect the varieties of psychological problems. Contemporary fascination with cost-effective and evidence-based treatments acquire credence because they assume that only certain kinds of psychological problems merit attention. Evidence-based practice seems best suited to disorders, such as schizophrenia or obsessive compulsive disorder, and fits less well disorganised or fragmented mental distress, especially if this is rooted in psycho-social difficulties in daily living. The implication, perhaps, is that the latter are unworthy of the professional expertise of therapists. Since the NHS has accepted the concept of scarcity, it is now acceptable to raise questions about the appropriateness of some psychiatric patient groups. When, in the past, evidence has been cited to show that community psychiatric nurses have few psychotic patients among their caseloads, this evidence has also had the implicit effect of casting doubt on the   validity of such caseloads, giving rise to concepts of patients who are seriously and enduringly mentally ill. Correspondingly, patients whose problems are less explicit, less measurable, are identified as worried, but essentially well; equally the nature of their problems, grounded as they are in their personal narrative, does not lend itself to any easily comprehensible evidence base or outcomes.

Institutionalism

But Bannister was surely right to argue that only by valuing the personal—and he is historically correct here as well—can we hope to mount challenges to institutional forms of care. For institutional psychiatry is littered with abuse; by institutional psychiatry, we mean not just inpatient asylums and hospitals, but the litanies of corrosive attitudes and practices that have characterised much of institutional provision (Martin, 1984). We believe that the findings presented here re-inforce this historical picture, and we suggest that, ultimately, too close an adherence to one type of (quantitative) evidence will deprive patients of the benefits they might accrue from help based on other perspectives. No-one should easily set aside questions about the nature of evidence or the importance to practice of different kinds of evidence. After all, if 'the evidence' points to the efficacy of a particular psychoactive drug that does not mean that administering the drug is without ethical issue: its refusal by a detained patient, for instance, does not mean that the refusal should be set aside: for the refusal is as much evidence to be taken into account as is the pharmacological indication for giving the drug. Classical (institutional) psychiatry, of course, sets aside patients' refusals as irrelevant: such refusals are seen as indicating the clinical phenomenon 'non compliance'.

Bannister went on to say that 'if our experience of psychological therapy makes sense to us, that is to say we can see reasons why we have been of no help to this person, or some help to that person, and we find that we can develop and elaborate our understanding through our work, we are likely to continue to work this way *whatever* the literature may say' (p219 his italics). Commenting on Bannister's paper, Miller Mair (1998) said: 'this little piece should be required reading for people in all professions engaging in therapeutic conversation. I especially like the last paragraph, which reads':

> *'My contention is that we should work as psychologists not as psychic paramedics. Our language, research methods and theory should be drawn from psychology and not from an imprisoning imitation of medical treatment studies' (p220).*

If true for psychologists, how doubly true this is for psychiatric nurses. Before moving on, we would like to labour the point that we are not contending that therapists—be they doctors or otherwise—avoid forming relationships in their work. Our point is that it is insulting to denigrate those who do this for its own sake, to minimise the value of work which falls outside empirical forms of reductive research or tangible evidence bases.

Mixtures

For nurses seeking enhanced scientific standing, one tendency is to opt for multidisciplinary research, research that complements other professions including, of course, medicine [see Ritter (1997) for an exposition of this position]. According to Miller and Crabtree (2000), nurses should embrace a mixture of qualitative and quantitative strands: qualitative approaches to examine such things as context, meaning, power, and complexity and quantitative approaches to provide measurements and a focussed anchor. These strands would be united by the nature of the research questions 'creating codes of understanding as they mutually pick apart difficult issues of patient care'. Miller and Crabtree include an example to show how both approaches coalesce, but which also slyly indicates the deficiencies of quantitative work whenever social complexities enter the scene. They refer to Jolly *et al* (1998) who examined a nurse-led programme relating to helping heart attack victims maintain a rehabilitation programme and improve health habits. Using RCT methods, their study yielded statistically insignificant results: however, when Wiles (1998) conducted qualitative interviews with 25 of the participants at various intervals, several findings pertaining to the acquisition and loss of trust were deemed to be clinically valuable.

The use of triangulation (different approaches) is interesting, but it misses an important point, which is that nurse researchers may be mistaken in striving to emulate scientific research. This also happens when they construct their qualitative investigations in such a way as to make them 'read' like 'proper' research studies. So, instead of validity and reliability, we are presented with erudite discussions about 'creditability' or 'authenticity' and so on. Equally, it is often asserted that qualitative research should proceed as a kind of preliminary exercise that unearths factors and material, which can then, presumably, be subjected to 'real' (i.e. quantitative) analysis. Even when psychiatric nursing models—the Tidal Model recently propounded by Professor Phil Barker and his team (Barker, 2000) is a good example—place the patient's experience at the centre of attention, they are still minded to insist that their work is evidence-based. In Loewenthal's (1999) view, these qualitative preoccupations with 'results' and 'outcomes' are still to do with objective thought, still wrapped up in the scientific world view. Whereas, for people who are troubled psychologically, the emphasis ought to be on the feeling state: Loewenthal draws on Kierkegaard (1941: 67) to make the point:

> 'While objective thought is indifferent to the thinking subject and his existence, the subjective thinker is an existing individual essentially interested in his own thinking, existing as he does in thought. His thinking has, therefore, a different type of reflection, namely the reflection of inwardness, of possession, by virtue of which it belongs to the thinking subject and no one else. While objective thought translates everything into results, and helps all mankind to cheat, by copying these off and reciting

them by rote, subjective thought puts everything in process and omits the result: partly because this belongs to him who has the way, and partly because, as an existing individual, he is constantly in the process of coming to be, which holds true of every human being who has not permitted himself to be deceived into becoming objective'.

This is essentially the position exemplified in the 1960s and 1970s by British radical psychiatry (Laing, 1960; Laing and Esterson, 1964) and which has been firmly discarded by conventional psychiatry that increasingly favours bio-chemical explanations. Psychiatric nurses are probably too large and heterogeneous a group to settle for any one set of explanations: many will favour the medical route, but some will also hanker after broader-based responses. Given what we present here of the current state of inpatient service delivery, we think that considerable room remains for a social analysis of psychiatric care, which includes both professionals' and patients' perspectives. It is true that some patients have lost their capacity for objective thought: however, this loss is, subjectively, who they are and these people are worthy of a more comprehensive, humane consideration than that which they have traditionally received. The Hearing Voices Network is testimony (evidence?) of the denial of patients' voices, by which we mean the subjective experience of those voices. Nurses have played their fair share in this denial, but probably because they have allowed themselves to be cast in a secondary, intermediary role to medicine and the general management of wards. Perhaps the demand that nurses supply evidence in support of what they do will inspire them to define their work and its efficacy in terms of patient care. To that end, attention needs to be paid to what counts as evidence: a degree of scepticism about the nature of evidence, as well as the potential self-ishness of its application, might allow nurses a broader, protective take on patients' welfare.

Chapter 3
The method of inquiry

*T*he aim of this project was to gain a better understanding of psychiatric nursing practice in the acute inpatient setting. As mentioned in our introduction, this environment is often chaotic and stressful, prone to external pressures and with the nursing focus unclear, the evidence base underpinning practice being potentially diverse. During discussions with the project steering group, it was agreed that, in order to account for these factors and gain a richer understanding of their connectedness, a methodology that would allow us to explore individual experiences and perspectives was needed, especially in the contexts concerned. Porter (in Cormack, 1991: 330) states that:

'qualitative analysis is concerned with describing the actions and interactions of research subjects in a certain context, and with interpreting the motivations and understandings that lie behind their actions'.

A more comprehensive description was provided by Cobb and Hagermaster (1987) who also stated that qualitative research is a type of investigation in which there is:

1. An attention to the social context in which events occur and have meaning;

2. An emphasis on understanding the social world from the viewpoint of the participants in it; and

3. An approach which is primarily inductive.

In addition, they also noted that important data collecting techniques include:

4. Interviewing, participant observation, examination of personal documents and other printed materials; and that

5. Qualitative research is primarily about discovery and description.

In this type of research, specific hypotheses tend to be set aside in favour of inductive processes whereby the researcher eschews, as far as possible, preconceptions about the unit or system under investigation. Instead, the unravelling 'story' of the area under review is observed and then reported back to the research audience. Analysis is presented for the large part in narrative rather than numerical form and it is assumed that the readers of this narrative will have some understanding of the area concerned.

The epistemology upon which such research is based 'is determined by the ethnographer' (Robertson and Boyle, 1984). Stern (1980) similarly declares that 'the investigator makes a choice regarding the relative salience of the problems under study'. These statements imply that different researchers will arrive at different conclusions about what the data means. Of course, since qualitative material is usually intended for an interested audience—what material is not?—then it cannot risk insulting its readership with interpretations that are unreal, fanciful, or idiosyncratic. Indeed, qualitative researchers comprise a research mindedness that acutely takes account of what counts as good, acceptable work. In effect, this self-conscious dependence on narrative forms provokes a fastidiousness both in evolving and describing terms of reference, including conclusions.

Virtually all qualitative research supports the contention that behaviour can only be understood in the context in which it occurs. Qualitative research seeks to describe experiences within natural settings, so as to generate ideas that might go some way towards explaining those experiences and their relationship to, in this instance, the kinds of nursing practice occurring within inpatient settings. This means developing investigative strategies to map out people's perceptions so as to codify, analyse, and donate them to whatever current knowledge base exists in the area under study. We can use Mischler's (1979) distinction between this approach and the more traditional scientific method to show how they differ.

Quantitative (scientific) studies

1. Outside observer: separate from phenomenon being studied
2. Seeks one truth to explain a phenomenon
3. Interested in causal relationships
4. Context stripping assumptions and numerical methods

Qualitative

1. Observer and phenomenon often intertwined
2. Many different but equal truths depending on the purpose and focus of the investigation
3. Seeks an understanding of the meaning of phenomena: searches for human experience
4. Analysis is inductive and holistic

Aggleton and Chalmers (1986) comment on the tension that exists between these two orientations. The utility of the scientific method within the natural and medical sciences has given it a status, which those keen on evidence-based practice often perceive as lacking in other approaches. Ludemann (1979), for instance, notes that qualitative work is often seen as 'somehow second class, and a little less than scientific'.

For this study, we believed that a qualitative approach based on participant observation, semi-structured interviews, and documentary analysis would allow pertinent issues to emerge and be interpreted in a progressive and consultative way. While the potential for theory generation was considered, it was agreed that the project should primarily provoke discussion in relation to problems of actual practice.

Initial stages

The initial stage of the project involved undertaking an extensive literature review to gain a better understanding of the inpatient setting, psychiatric nursing as practised in this environment, the evidence base relating to practice with psychotic patients, and the policy and legislative frameworks encompassing the whole area.

Contact was made with identified project leads in each area so that the varied nature of the services would be better understood. Networks with other senior clinicians and academics were also established locally to provide broader perspectives on the local picture. Access was negotiated with the local project leaders and the project was introduced to the ward teams during 'handovers', as well as through informal contacts with staff.

The possible inclusion of patients in this project was discussed at length with the steering group. Despite the perceived vulnerability of mental health patients, it is still imperative that their views be sought within the research process, especially when there is a paucity of understanding of patient 'perspectives'; in the context of this project, however, we felt that there was sufficient extant information on patients' perspectives in existing studies, for example 'Acute Problems' (Sainsbury, 1988) and 'Environmentally Friendly' (Baker, 2000). It was, therefore, agreed that patient feedback would not be directly elicited, but if offered spontaneously could be used as deep background to the study. In light of this, we did not feel that formal ethical approval from the hospital trusts concerned was needed.

Beginnings

A period of 4–6 weeks was spent in each of the five services. An initial period of participant observation was followed by semi-structured interviews with qualified staff. Melia (1982) stated that the nature of the participant's perspective in participant observation depended largely on the researcher's experience of the setting under review. In this study, the participant project worker had an intimate knowledge of the inpatient setting and this was communicated to the ward teams in the initial period of engagement. Melia further remarks that participant observation places the emphasis on the researcher in the generation of data. Throughout the initial period of participant observation, the project worker aimed to interpret and give meaning to the phenomena observed through the perspective of those being observed, and data was generated by means of interactions between the project worker and the participants.

Polit and Hungler (1993) defined two methods of recording data from participant observation:

1. A daily log which records conversations and events that have taken place; and

2 Field notes that are not only a record of events, but also a preliminary attempt to analyse their meaning.

As Lofland and Lofland (1984: 62) note: 'For better or worse, the human mind forgets massively and quickly'. As such, making field notes became essential for both transcription and analysis.

Participant observation took place predominantly between nine and five o'clock, Monday to Friday, because this allowed two shifts to be observed as well as permitting involvement in handovers and other staff meetings. In other words, this was the busiest time on the wards when other professionals and ancillary staff were usually around. Time was spent in the nursing office and communal areas on the wards. Nursing notes and other documentation, such as books, journals, notice boards, and similar sources of information were also viewed during these observation periods.

Although participant observation and interviews are separate approaches, the literature has often depicted observation as the primary method (Becker and Geer, 1960). Ragucci (1972) holds that: 'The method of participant observation is synonymous with the ethnographic approach' (p487).

Similarly, Lofland (1976) regards participant observation as the yardstick against which other methods are compared. However, Schatzman and Strauss (1973) question this dichotomy and Lofland and Lofland (1984: 13) regard the distinction as overdrawn, quoting West (1980) that:

'...the bulk of participant observation data is probably gathered through informal interviews and supplemented by observation.'

and that: a 'mutuality of both methods are the central techniques of the naturalistic investigator'.

The role of the observer

Bruyn (1970) notes that the role of participant observer runs counter to the observer in the natural sciences who remains neutral. He notes the danger of the qualitative researcher being changed by his data, so that the research process involves a consistent effort to remain unchanged to ensure that he can analyse and report findings relatively objectively.

> 'the issue is not whether he will become emotionally involved, but rather the nature of the involvement. The involvement, whether it is closer to one end of the continuum (sympathetic identification) or the other end (projective distortion), is very little a function of an observer's role. Rather, it is primarily a function of his experience, awareness, and personality constellation and the way these become integrated with a particular situation. Sympathetic identification includes empathic communication and imaginative participation in the life of the observed through identification and role taking. In this type of involvement the observer is both detached and affectively participating; he feels no need to moralise or judge the interaction; his attitude is one of interested curiosity and matter-of-fact inquiry directed towards understanding the observed.'

(Schwartz and Schwartz, 1955; in Bruyn, 1970: 306)

In effect, the researcher cannot enter the social world of his subjects, since this kills his objectivity; instead, he keeps his identity vague thus avoiding social alignment; he remains marginal and, while this affects the kind of data he will reveal, it allows him to act on that data with a reasonable degree of confidence. This is necessary if meaning is to be attributed to a subject's statements and actions. Over time, however, and allowing for a relatively high degree of inter-relating with subjects, the level of marginality (of the researcher) becomes redefined, so that the extent to which he can participate and, at the same time, remain detached provides a basis for tackling the problem of validity. For example, observer contamination of subjects by over identification or familiarity would constitute a violation of internal validity (Germain, 2001). The central concern in this study was to avoid just such contamination, since most writers agree that the presence of researchers distorts the natural field of the system being measured. However, such concerns are appropriate and may even serve the investigation. As Lofland and Lofland (1984) note: 'The constant worrying about this problem protects against its actual occurrence'.

Field and Morse (1985) note that the close relationship of researchers to the data generated in participant observation is also present when collecting data from informal interviews. Sapsford and Abbott (1992) describe interviews as enabling informants to give their views in their own terms: it is important that the researcher avoids imposing her own ideas on the conversation as much as possible. The initial part of the project had highlighted specific areas for consideration and the interview schedule of questions reflected this. We had fully expected that nursing interactions with psychotic patients would be observed and that the interviews would allow an opportunity for exploring the nature of these interactions. However, it quickly became apparent that such interactions were not happening with sufficient regularity to form a basis for interview questions. It was necessary to formulate questions that would allow nurses to describe their practice in a realistic, but uncontrived manner.

In total, seven questions were asked, with follow up questions, prompts, or slight variations depending on the individual being interviewed. The questions were as follows:

1. Can you tell me a bit about yourself, how long you've been qualified, what you've been doing since?

2. Which patients do you prefer/feel most comfortable working with?

3. Which patients do you least prefer/feel least comfortable working with?

4. When a patient is admitted who is described as psychotic, what approaches do you find most useful/are you likely to use?

5. Have you had any training that has prepared you for working with psychotic patients?

6. Have you had any role models/other learning opportunities?

7. Have you read or heard about any interesting research/practice developments?

Throughout both processes (of observations and interviews), the closeness of the researcher to her subjects was self-monitored and constantly kept under review. Questions were open-ended and allowed informants to describe their own thoughts and feelings freely, and nurses were informed that the content of their interviews would be represented anonymously.

As is typically the case with observations and interviews, a huge amount of data was generated, and attributing meaning and value to it became a complex (and prolonged) process. Buckeldee and McMahon (1994) describe an 'analysis mire', with researchers working through an inordinate amount of material in order to gain some understanding of its meaning. In our case, however, the process was facilitated by supervision and discussion within the steering group; this forum provided a vehicle for the exploration of findings and the proposition of initial inferences on a more formal level, and this was supplemented by informal discussions with colleagues and networking contacts.

Analysing the data

The following processes were considered when analysing the data. Glaser and Strauss (1967) describe the process of 'constant comparative analysis' where data collection and analysis proceed concurrently so that codes, categories, and themes are generated and developed as they are progressively compared with incoming data. An adaptation of this strategy provided the following systematic approach for analysing data:

1. Collection of empirical data;

2. Concept formation: code the data—cluster the codes into initial small categories;

3. Concept and theme development: collapse these small categories into larger categories; and

4. Concept modification and theme integration: encapsulate these large categories into themes which explain the phenomena.

It is such strategies that constitute the emerging challenge of qualitative studies, but the studies are then criticised as lacking objectivity. Qualitative investigators respond that their work is more scientific than the positivist tradition, since they see it as more 'socially valid'. For example, they say that quantitative social science has failed to make concepts 'intelligible and clear' because of an attachment to hypothetico-deductive schemas, and that the use of these in social research has led to such grotesque parodies (of science) that the study of human action has been almost completely crippled (Crick, 1976). In plain language, attempts to bring scientific equations into human relationships, inevitably and necessarily, demean them such that, ultimately, they become meaningless. Qualitative research as such owes its very existence to methods that generate narrative as opposed to statistical material. The success of the positivist tradition relies instead upon a mathematical idiom, together with an inherent distaste for a 'science' couched in the language of everyday life. The choice facing social science investigators thus falls between mathematical or semantic styles of investigation. Certainly, were we to dispense with the semantic resources of ordinary language in our work, we would produce little more than nonsense descriptions of human behaviour. People normally say what is on their minds, as well as express attitudes towards their surroundings be this a betting shop or psychiatric ward. To ignore their views, or to subvert them by transforming them to numerical or other physical data seems perverse (Burns and Grove, 2001). At the same time, Silverman (1989) drawing upon Foucault (1977), makes the point that our twentieth century preoccupation with language fails to explain meaning because it ignores the 'homogenizing' strength of institutions. But it is here that qualitative investigations come into their own, in that they can take account of the intermingling of social systems and the individuals who inhabit them. In the present study, the inhibiting effects of psychiatric wards and their rituals is made explicit in relation to the nurses' ability to function as agents of care. The interplay of individuals and their organisations is complex, and the extent to which 'the whole differs from the sum of its parts' becomes: To what extent are the nurses in this study responsible for their conditions of work? To what extent might they formulate an alternative language or strategies to offset the indeterminate (but pervasive) weight of institutionalised practices?

Meaning

We can identify language in terms of its use between persons (Wittgenstein, 1968). However, in our case, the meaning may be seen as coming from frameworks where the determining factor is power; either power in the roles that people inhabit, or in the various elements that go to make up their institutions. Yet power only partly stems from language (Etzioni, 1960) so that analyses of institutions cannot be reduced to subjects' statements. While subjects may share some meanings, not all institutional processes will reflect meanings owned by the staff ensemble in equal proportion. Which is to say, some subjects will possess power (hierarchical or otherwise) that will determine the relative influence of their statements and *some will not*. Sharp (1975) quotes Gouldner (1971) to develop the point that it is not only when power is brutal—when it is poised to express itself as a force—that its presence is sensed in social relationships and generates motives for *willing* obedience. Power also exists quietly, as it were, and is fully real even at lower ranges of intensity. Power, in short, exists not simply when authority breaks down; it exists as a factor in the life of subordinates, shaping their behaviour and beliefs at every moment of their relations with those above them. The obvious inference is that conclusions based upon analyses of verbal statements may simply represent personal perspectives: unsupported by other (external) data such conclusions may appear fragile. The descriptions presented in subsequent chapters of this book reflect not just the assertions of the nurses involved, but also our systematic observation and mapping of their behaviours, as they struggle to construct a viable working role within prohibitive acute psychiatric ward settings.

Positivism the norm?

Before considering this approach in more detail, a consideration of quantitative research might also provide some insight into why we chose alternative methods. The quantitative approach derives from a Popperian philosophy that aims to verify causal relationships within existing theories: knowledge is acquired via a building blocks process of itemising and extracting variables (from their natural context or culture) and subjecting them to experimental processes of hypothesis formation, analysis of causal relationships and deductive reasoning, and statistical evaluation of outcomes (Popper, 1959). The extraction of causal relationships between variables is typically the goal, with minimal attention to the subjective experiences of the subjects involved. This has promoted the view that the positivist stance starves the outcomes of enquiry of their meaning, that experimental designs sacrifice meaning so as to meet the assumptions of their paradigm, what Liam Hudson (1966) refers to as 'Methodolatry'. Trenchantly, Shotter (1975) has personified this as man '...buried under the debris of our own investigations'.

Generally, this research is taught as procedures of data collection and analysis, where social facts are seen as external to individuals and thus amenable to objective study. People act according to social facts or laws and not according to their psychological motives. Naturally, where categorised social facts are given numerical form, statistical correlations become possible or even, in some cases, causal connections.

> *'All advances of scientific understanding at every level begin with a speculative adventure, an imaginary preconception of what might be true—a preconception which always, and necessarily, goes a little way (sometimes a long way) beyond anything which we have logical or factual authority to believe in. It is the invention of a possible world, or of a tiny fraction of that world. The conjecture is then exposed to criticism to find out whether or not that imagined world is anything like the real one. Scientific reasoning is, therefore, at all levels an interaction between two episodes of thought—a dialogue between two voices, the one imaginative and the other critical; a dialogue, if you like, between what might be true and what is in fact the case.'*

(Medawar, 1972; cited in Cohen *et al*, 2000: 14)

What 'might be true' is expressed as the hypothesis of the study and this introduces a predictive element into research, which is also anticipated as a numerical level of significance. Rigour and testability are 'de rigueur' particularly in the quest for falsification of the hypothesis. For this is a paradigm that:

> *'...does not yield absolute or eternal truth, but rather systematic doubt; it reduces uncertainty rather than producing absolute knowledge. And it [can] only [answer] questions of a factual nature.'*

(Jehu, 1972; cited in Herbert, 1990: 15)

Positivist deficiencies

Positivist approaches can be criticised on two counts: firstly, the method of systematic doubt can be seen to trivialise science, especially when these methods are applied to social affairs; secondly, asserting that the scientific method is the only legitimate pathway to truth is arrogant. Popkewitz (1984) identifies traces of ideology here, with the shift from science to dogma embracing a series of flaws:

1. Commitment to rigorous techniques at the expense of theoretical interests by stressing those aspects of the research that can be numerically described;

2. Objectivity is narrowly defined and, paradoxically, data is stripped of human values so as to facilitate the development of laws of human nature. Statistical manipulation is used to achieve this and some techniques may be procedurally, but not philosophically well grounded; and

3. The emphasis on techniques may lead to problems that conform to the techniques: for instance, the distribution of data in a defined manner. The efforts that go towards improving the techniques of science lead to a neglect of the assumptions underpinning these procedures.

Granted, procedurally defined techniques exist because a particular definition of science has given rise to them: equally, the emphasis on numerical components of research is seen as necessary so as to tightly control data and replicate it. But these expectations are hardly reasonable when inquiries focus on people's experiences in situations that are presumed to be— in this case—detrimental to their mental health. In our view, if nurses are to conduct research into the social settings of psychiatric care, then they must immerse themselves in the practice world: because induction, intuition, and psychological reflection are innate to practice, the investigative frameworks of nurses should normally be characterised by qualitative procedures.

Validity and reliability

Firstly, we must distinguish between external validity, which is the 'generalisability of a proposition about a causal relationship between populations' (Cook and Campbell, 1979) and internal validity, which is the examination of an evolving theory that, simultaneously, is used to describe variables under exploration, and the degree to which these variables support whatever theories the researchers might have about the field under study. The latter approach is the one most characterised by qualitative studies. Yet qualitative studies have never quite cast aside their preoccupation with external validity and reliability, and what this preoccupation has done is intensify the use of 'rough analogues' (of validity and reliability) that consist of trying to establish both the 'adequacy' of evidence as well as its 'credibility'. Factors that interfere with internal validity include:

1. Historical antecedents leading up to the research;

2. Changing relationships between subjects and researcher;

3. Subject mortality;

4. Differences between those studied and those not studied;

5. The reactive effects of the presence of the researcher; and

6. Contamination of the researcher by the unit under study.

Factors that improve internal validity include the constant comparative method, as well as the typically lengthy periods of data collection, observations, interviews, etc. Chenitz (1986) adds that the use of different approaches, for example observations and interviews, increases internal validity, since data obtained by one method is verified by cross-checking with another. However, without doubt, the question of external validity has been minimised through the use of 'credibility', 'evidence', and 'auditability' as analogous terms. While somewhat ambiguous and potentially misleading, these terms betray a genuine concern with issues of replicability in research.

Reliability

Qualitative methods also create difficulties in establishing reliability in research, difficulties that may be attributed to the individualistic techniques employed. Data gathering, for example, often involves complex intermingling of observations and interviews: communities, such as the ones investigated here, are always dynamic, rarely static, and data necessarily often has to be collected over lengthy time periods.

Recall at this point that the Popperian approach seeks to deduce evidence that will cast doubt on the hypothesis with which the investigation started out. Qualitative analysis, alternatively, seeks to unearth information that will support or enlighten existing ideas about what might be happening (and why) in a particular unit. In that sense, the tendency for qualitative studies to formulate 'new' categories of information from data, which contradicts existing ideas (rather than abandoning it), constitutes a radical departure from traditional (scientific) methods. The fact is that, in qualitative work where emerging properties contradict prevalent ideas, the tendency is to 're-create' the contradictory ideas as 'new categories': only rarely are categories abandoned, since to abandon new information would challenge the core of what qualitative research is. Yet discarding information because it fails to fit hardly serves the veracity of the study, if its central justification is the recognition that what matters is each person's account. Against this, Field and Morse (1985) refer to spurious inferences resulting from observer idiosyncrasies even in well-controlled studies, despite agreement existing about the appropriateness of qualitative work, confusion and (misplaced) confidence abound. In their view, this is because rival proposals, models, and terminologies are produced only to be quickly overtaken. They believe that the field is developing in the absence of coherent or agreed frames of reference.

Personal perspectives

Setting aside these criticisms, Quint (1967) and Ragucci (1972) state that in the accurate and detailed description of a point of view, a social world is the major contribution of qualitative research. When describing social systems, however, a tendency to impose form and meaning may prove irresistible. Often, it can feel as if the meaning, which qualitative researchers give to their data, significantly defines it such that what we are often left with are privileged insider's accounts.

Yet it is studies like these which have brought about greater social and political change than that achieved by more detached, numerical accounts in the sociological and psychiatric journals. While it could be said that scientific research is about facts and accuracy, it can equally be said that, where human welfare is at stake, a case exists for types of research whose aim is to improve people's lot by enlarging what we know about their situation (Porter, 2000).

It may be that distinguishing qualitative studies from more positivist accounts could limit the 'scientific respect', sought by many qualitative researchers. Researchers in this field differ on this: some seek to develop analogues that highlight the similarities between their own and quantitative studies. Others are less concerned to ape traditional approaches and accept that their work cannot be replicated, but that it does extend knowledge and familiarity of the research areas, that, with caution, can allow conclusions to be applied beyond the terrain where the research was done. Finally, as is the case here, where other previous reports also reveal similar findings, we may feel confident on a 'no smoke without fire' basis that our conclusions reflect current trends in people's thinking. It may not be physics or chemistry, but only an extreme sceptic would ignore the testimony of people whose occupational lives are on the line.

Chapter 4
Nurse-patient interactions

*D*uring this study, a total of 40 interactions were observed between nurses and patients. Of these, 29 were categorised as crisis or reactive responses where nurses responded to expressed needs in an immediate or opportunistic manner. Only 11 interactions could be categorised as planned or pro-active where the intervention related to a documented plan or a plan discussed with the therapeutic team and/or the patient. Naturally, the nature and timing of pro-active interactions were more considered and controlled than the *ad hoc* varieties. Nevertheless, it was crisis and reactive responses that largely characterised the nurse's activities.

Crisis/reactive interactions

On one occasion, a patient displays suspicious and confrontational behaviour towards the ward manager. The patient asserts that the ward manager has been involved in some kind of conspiracy against her. The patient is unwilling to accept that the ward manager is who she says she is and continues to insist, fairly aggressively, that she has been involved in some plan against her. The manager remains calm and non-confrontational and the patient eventually drops the subject.

I sit at the table where an adjacent patient states: 'God has asked him to sit next to him forever'. One of the nurses tries to explore this with him, but he becomes guarded and asks why he is being asked questions. The nurse explains that they want to understand a bit more about what he is saying and experiencing. But the patient remains suspicious and a little hostile.

Another patient comes to the ward office, dressed bizarrely, clutching several objects, a flower, an ashtray and a cup. She talks to a staff nurse who afterwards says 'she's convinced I have a partner called Fred. I don't challenge these beliefs anymore. She trusts me; we get on OK, I've known her for years.' The patient again comes to the ward office and accuses staff of stealing her leather skirt. She is angry and focusses on one nurse in particular: this is quite anxiety provoking for everybody, since this patient had to be restrained the previous day after biting a nurse's finger. The nurse quietly reassures her and offers to go and look for the skirt with her. The patient refuses and storms out of the office.

In some instances, interactions occurred because the ward was quiet and so staff became more available. The following two examples show how reactive responses and 'play it by ear' approaches can have positive outcomes; in these cases, considerable skill and understanding was demonstrated by the nurses concerned.

On a late shift, an informal patient, on the telephone, becomes increasingly angry and begins shouting about being 'fitted up' and that people are trying to make out that he is mad. He has informed some nurses that he is about to discharge himself. He is informal, but the nurses are concerned about his mental state, describing him as paranoid even if generally well contained. The patient becomes even more angry and when a female nurse approaches him he turns his anger on her. He moves very close to her shouting and gesticulating and demanding to know if she thinks he's mad. He says he's had enough and is going home to sort everything out when a second female nurse arrives and persuades him to wait and see a doctor. She takes him to a side room, talks to him, manages to persuade him to stay and take some medication. Both nurses know him and approach him quietly and calmly, accepting his anger, but also addressing his uncertainty, encouraging him to calm down and re-think things. They reassure him they do not think he is mad and state that they understand him 'having had enough'. Both nurses support each other, one doing the talking while the other provides a quiet presence. The situation is resolved before a doctor arrives. Afterwards they discuss what might have happened had they failed to persuade him to stay. Both agree he was detainable, but that it would have been dangerous to try and prevent him leaving.

The second example is of a patient standing at the entrance of one of the wards, refusing to come in, and attempting to get people to sign a petition against his detention. Yesterday, apparently, he 'went ballistic' and, the day before that, had gone absent without official leave and walked to town 30 miles away. Since being returned by the police he had been confined to the ward and had become increasingly agitated, threatening to strike some nurses with a stick. The police were called and, in their presence, he was medicated. The doctor on duty insisted that he be transferred to a low security environment. The nurses didn't agree saying that since he had responded to the medication it would be better for him if they could nurse him on the ward. They agree that he was very ill, but that they could continue to manage him.

I asked the nurse if they had completed a risk assessment which they hadn't. However, they felt that even had they done a risk assessment, it would make no difference to the doctor's intentions. The patient was placed on 'loose level one', an observation regime designated as 'not too obtrusive, but making sure the patient doesn't go anywhere'. There is, in fact, no care plan in the patient's documentation and no formal risk assessment. By next day, the patient has settled, is now calm and able to discuss with the nurses the concerns which they have about his behaviour. He has not been moved to a low security unit and he continues to be compliant with his medication. Despite a lack of formal assessment and a documented care plan, the team believe they have responded effectively and that the outcome is satisfactory to all concerned. The charge nurse says the patient was finding it difficult to cope with his existing restrictions, but that had he been transferred to a security unit it would have made him worse.

In the following examples, reactive responses are more about the nurses 'not being bothered' or are concerned with them trying to ensure a desired outcome, such as hospital discharge, or in making sure that detained patients remain on the ward.

After a handover, a patient came into the office expressing concern about flashing in his eyes and asking for help. He was advised to go and lie on his bed. About an hour later he asks me about it while I am sitting with him in the lounge. He doesn't know that I am not a member of staff, but he is obviously still worried about it and the nurses haven't dealt it with it.

While some nurses sit in the office, several patients come to the door, sometimes with specific requests that are dealt with there and then. For example, one patient asks to talk to someone and a nurse leaves the office, but doesn't get further than the corridor where she talks briefly with him before returning.

One patient is due to be discharged. According to some of the nurses she doesn't want to go, but they are keen to see her discharged. She is behaving quite bizarrely. She clutches objects to her (flower vase, teddy bear) and wanders about the ward in a disorientated state. The nurses interpret this as her 'building up to something' in order to prevent her imminent discharge. They are concerned that the medical staff will not stick with the agreed plan if and when she starts 'acting out'. Their view is that she has few options left: they know that her family are fed up with her and she has been thrown out of her accommodation. They suspect that she sees hospital as one of her better options and that she does not actually need psychiatric care. They deliberately do not respond to her so as to avoid her saying or doing anything that would compromise her discharge, but her behaviour seems to be causing concerns to other patients who try and talk to her or approach the nurses on her behalf.

A male patient absconds. Alarms go off. About four nurses chase after him and he is forcibly returned to the ward. Some staff appear to be exhilarated one of them saying that they caught the patient 'by the scruff of his neck'. Escorted to and left in his room, no subsequent time or support is offered him and when I ask about this, I am told that he is detained under Section 3 of the Mental Health Act with a diagnosis of paranoid schizophrenia and that he usually presents as being very suspicious, non-communicative and truculent.

The character and style of these interactions define much of what passed between the nurses and their patients with the nurses appearing to act as sounding boards for the myriad complaints, demands, needs, desires and persecutions of their patients. Visibly, their capacity to absorb and deal with the barrage of problems was limited and so they developed a range of avoidance (of patients) tactics, seemingly designed to protect and defend their own mental stability. While it seems inconceivable that anyone could remain actively therapeutic for a full nursing shift of eight hours, such was the comprehensiveness of the pressures on the nurses, it became difficult for many of them to maintain a modest pretence of therapeutic engagement, even for short periods of time.

Planned/proactive interactions

This sub-theme considered nurse-initiated interactions that had been previously planned as evidenced by documentation, team discussion and/or discussions with patients. Because interactions of this type took place in side-rooms, they were not directly observed as such. In some instances, we identified the nature of these encounters from patient's notes and they appeared to occur mostly in the evenings or at weekends when, presumably, more time was available. Significantly, during 200 hours of observation, only eight planned interactions appeared to take place. For example, three patients diagnosed with borderline personality disorder were offered one-to-one time on a regular basis. Their primary nurse agreed to see them once per shift (when on duty) and their allocated nurse also agreed to offer them 10–15 minutes per shift at other times. Another instance of planned interventions related to a patient with a history of paranoid schizophrenia. This patient's notes showed evidence of the implementation of specific relapse prevention strategies; for example, attempting to identify early warning signs and the organisation of a support group. The notes also showed that this patient had read and signed his care plan.

However, the formulation of care plans from which there then flowed therapeutic activities by nurses was not a common occurrence. The problem appeared to relate to traditions that locked the nurses into responsibilities and obligations to the myriad problems of patients, the majority of which were only tenuously linked to their psychiatric illnesses. While other professional disciplines seemed able to focus on the clinical status of patients, and thus avoid any involvement in their wider concerns, the nurses had assumed, somehow, a housekeeper or (even) parental answerability for their overall situations.

Patient behaviours

It was observed that particular patient behaviours elicited different responses from the nursing staff, as well as having an impact upon the ward as a whole. Certain behaviours attracted attention, while others went unnoticed. Ignoring some patients resulted from the general busyness of the wards and was not necessarily a free choice by the nurses concerned. Whereas responses seemed to be forthcoming when patient's behaviours became disruptive or if someone's behaviour presented a risk, such as when patients became aggressive or when they tried to leave the unit: in such cases the nurses reacted immediately.

> One patient is in the process of being detained and awaits a visit from her social worker. In the meantime, she remains legally informal and so cannot be medicated, restrained, or forcibly treated in any way. Other patients are either frightened or angry because she is so disruptive: she is in the 'smoke room' shouting at another patient who shoves her out of the way. A staff nurse approaches her, but this only inflames the situation and she now begins screaming. She remains very angry and argumentative. The nurses decide to remove her to her room and ring for assistance from another ward. In the end, four nurses go into the smoke room, persuade the other patients to (reluctantly) leave and then escort the patient out. In the event, she leaves calmly and is subsequently given oral medication. All of the nurses have been involved in dealing with this incident, which has lasted for almost two hours. Although the other patients are distressed by the incident, the nurses have been unable to deal with them having focussed their energies on the disruptive patient.

> There are four substance misuse/alcoholic patients on ward who have created significant problems over the weekend. One of them has been very threatening and demanding that he be given medication. When he doesn't get it, he begins to throw furniture around the ward. A junior doctor is reluctant to discharge him and this provokes a round of discussion with the medical and community alcohol teams to see if a discharge can be organised. In fact, the medical team are reluctant to see him go, but the nurses are adamant that he be transferred out.

What is notable is the extent to which one patient is able to dominate a ward's atmosphere by creating an aura of tension and apprehension. Significantly, the nursing response seems to be less about formulating a therapeutic response and more about administratively organising the patient's discharge. Once this had been achieved, the atmosphere shifts and things start to calm down somewhat. Subsequently, in the confines of the ward office, the sense among the nurses is of having achieved a victory in bringing about the discharge of this resented patient.

> One patient is very loud, going in and out of the smoking and non-smoking lounges and seemingly unable to settle. At one point, he can be seen walking continuously around the outside of the building. Another patient is similarly unsettled as well as being over-talkative and especially inquisitive about who I am. The nurses are either in the office, clinic room, or in the dining room supervising meals and seem quite oblivious of these patient's behaviours.
>
> One patient has been loudly requesting inhalers all morning and complaining of not being able to breath. A nurse informs her that she must be able to breathe as she is 'managing to shout alright.' In the afternoon, a staff nurse says that the patient is, in fact, asthmatic and has been prescribed inhalers in the past. This nurse wants the doctor to see the patient because, she says, she 'can't be bothered to argue with her anymore'.

The capacity of the nurses to dismiss different kinds of patient's behaviours as unworthy of attention or further inquiry is perhaps surprising. Depending on the nature of these behaviours, the nursing response could even be abrasive, flippant or indifferent. On occasions, persistent 'nuisance' type behaviours would force the nurses into making judgmental responses.

> A young girl described as being manic appears very restless and frequently comes to the office door. She doesn't want anything in particular except to chat to the staff, asking them personal questions, such as 'are you married?' The nurses ignore her questions and ask her to leave.
>
> A second patient, described as an 'old chronic', repeatedly comes into the office and asks for a cigarette (which he has to do since the nurses retain his cigarettes so as to manage his tobacco

intake). He is allowed a cigarette every half hour, but as soon as he finishes it, he approaches the office to ask for another. He is reminded repeatedly when his next cigarette is due, but, nevertheless, continues to ask. He is verbally, brusquely, and physically prompted to leave the office. The latter took the form of grabbing him by the upper arms, abruptly turning him around, and pushing him out the door without any verbal interaction taking place.

A patient with very little English keeps coming to the office asking to use the phone. At the request of her family, she has been allowed two phone calls a day. On this occasion, she begins to shout loudly into the phone before slamming it down. She then comes to the office twice in the next 20 minutes wanting to make more calls. She is told she can't, but won't leave the office, so staff move to physically remove her. She comes back again and grabs at the phone. The phone is removed from her and she is physically removed from the office.

A patient comes to the office repeatedly because she wants to go home. For this, she requires an escort and the round trip will take nearly three hours. She is told that no staff are available that day and that the best they can do is the day after next. Despite this, she keeps coming back and repeating her need to go home: she needs, she says, to fetch some clothes and collect her mail. After it is again explained that no staff are available, she refuses to leave the office and when other nurses enter the office she restarts the process of asking to go home. In the end she is physically removed from the office.

A patient comes up to a nurse and asks if she looks alright. The nurse replies 'fine'. The patient then shows the nurse her nicotine discoloured fingers saying, 'look at my fingers', to which the nurse reminds her that she has suggested that she clean them with lemon juice. The patient asks again if she looks alright, but is asked to leave the office when a doctor arrives. The nurse informs me that this patient asks the same questions all day and is never reassured by the responses she gets. The patient sees the doctor enter the office and comes to ply him with her questions. He tells her to talk to the nurses about it. They, in turn, ask her to leave the office.

One male nurse discusses how he shoved a female patient out of the office after the patient had pushed him. He relates how the patient fell down when this happened. The story is told with much bravado and quite openly, with little apparent concern about the patient's well being. According to the nurse, this patient was annoying and is someone who deliberately tries to 'wind staff up'.

Something else that is notable is the number of patients who, although evidently distressed or in some kind of need, seem unable to communicate this to the nursing staff so that whatever is bothering them goes unnoticed. In some cases, some of these patients could be seen making an effort to communicate their feelings, but without obtaining any response from the nurses concerned. Administrative overload has already been mentioned as a reason for this, but it also seemed that the nurses discriminated between needs for which they might supply some tangible solution, for example, preventing emotional escalations, as opposed to needs that stemmed from experiential distress and for which—for whatever reason—they felt they could do little. The overall impression was of groups of nurses who were pragmatic rather than psychologically minded; addressing the ward's 'needs' and not the patients; specifically, addressing needs or events perceived by them as threatening to the ward environment, and giving second place to needs if they appeared irrelevant to the overall management of the ward.

One patient keeps coming out of his room and wandering along the corridor. He looks anxious, but because of the ward's design he cannot be seen by the office-bound nurses and so he ambles back to his room. Significantly, patient areas are not always observable from the nursing office.

Of course, this begs the question of whether they should be visible, and some former patients (Coleman, 1999) have complained about the lack of privacy that attended their psychiatric hospitalisation. Having said that, respecting patient's privacy as part of a contract based on trust, and not actually knowing at a given time what potentially vulnerable patients are doing are two different things.

In the communal lounge, I listened in to a conversation between two patients, one of whom doesn't know what the side effects of his drugs are. The other patient is telling him (erroneously) what his drugs are for. In the end, one of them goes and gets a leaflet that explains one of the drugs both of them are taking and they sit and read it together. Another patient then starts talking about his unhappiness at being hospitalised. He says that he has written to the chief executive of the hospital about this. He feels that he hasn't been able to get the information he wants. He addresses these complaints to me and two other patients who are no longer paying him any attention.

A patient comes into the ward office in mid-afternoon, obviously sedated and very sleepy, and asks if he has missed lunch. He is told that it is three o'clock and that lunch was at mid-day. He asks if anything has been saved for him. It hasn't.

As these examples show, patients are often left to their own devices for extensive periods of time and, in some instances, even basic requirements (such as ensuring that they had been fed) are not met. This 'air of neglect' is particularly notable whenever the nursing staff congregate in the ward office, a space for which they have a fair degree of reverence. Time and time again the nurses become visibly unnerved if patients enter this space, and they always seem keen to escort them back out into the communal ward areas. The sanctity of the office is especially prized during handovers and patients were fully expected to keep their distance during these periods.

The nurses are in a handover: one patient is watching over everything in the ward; she tells visitors where the staff are and helps other patients by making drinks for them. A second patient still tries to get cigarettes from the office, but no one is available to respond to her. The patients seem generally unsettled. There is a staff meeting after the handover and this leaves only one agency nurse managing the ward for nearly an hour.

It seems extraordinary that none of the nurses see anything unusual in retiring en masse to the office in order to have their handovers between shifts, that for considerable periods of time patients are left in the hands of an agency nurse, an auxiliary, or even another patient. This is not to suggest any easy way of 'handing over' each shift. What is interesting is the absence of any sense of this being a problem. Handover is seen as the essential tool of ward management; it accompanied the foundation of the Victorian asylums, with their dominant ethic of communal, custodial management, to become the standard medium of communication. The problem is that communal management sits uncomfortably within a contemporary ideology that places individual patients at the centre of care. This is the conundrum: how to construct a model that attends to the individual needs of patents within systems that originated in an earlier age when separation and custodial supervision were the norm.

Interviews

It was inevitable that these issues would surface in the interviews with the nursing staff, some of whom were quick to offer qualifying comments. The most common defence of non interactive nursing was 'lack of time': the ward was 'too busy, too often' and they were simply unable to focus on individual patients given the broader requirements of ward management. It was not their choice to neglect individual care in favour of administrative duties, but this was expected of them. Without doubt that expectation was the offspring of history—custom and practice—and so ingrained that even contemporary concepts of therapeutic nursing, as advocated by nurse educationalists and even some nursing managers, was insufficient to counteract the realities of inpatient services. Indeed, some nurses actively frowned on deviations from the mentality of 'running the ward' and were suspicious of that minority of nurses whose inclinations lay in the direction of individual counselling of patients.

A staff nurse stated:

'The other staff used to get angry about me spending time with one patient: we had sessions of one hour. There's a blame culture if you spend too much time on individual patients.'

In another staff nurse's view:

'The nursing assistants spend time with the patients that would be more appropriate for me to be spending with them. They play scrabble with them and paint their nails while all I do is deal with the most challenging aspects of their behaviour. You become de-skilled in non-confrontational interaction and if you

don't have that sort of interaction then you can't make good assessments and care plans.'

One staff nurse confessed:

'The last few weeks I have been fed up. I want to change direction. Its partly to get new skills, but its partly due to the things that patients present us with, mainly violence and intimidation. We have become victims of being too tolerant. There was a patient who made very serious threats against specific staff, but he couldn't be discharged without the consultant's permission. Another patient's relatives were very threatening to staff, threatening to kill them, but the police were unable to act. There's no respect for nurses. Its like its OK to threaten nurses.'

Unusually, one nurse declared a predilection for disruptive and difficult patients:

'I have always liked working with psychotics, but I like working with difficult clients too, like patient B. The other staff refer to her as that 'bloody woman'. She has a marginal personality disorder. She had a lot of trauma in her early life, then she met her husband and he rescued her. When he died a lot of things resurfaced. She can't cope. I like working with people like her, but it can be very intense and I have to avoid some patients because I have too much on anyway. Clients will still come and find me.'

In the main, however, the interviews turned on the question of how certain patients or particular behaviours monopolise nurse's time. Other constraints that connected with this were problems relating to patient mix. It wasn't difficult to see that, in addition to time constraints, with low staffing levels, and the managerial, routinised requirements of the nursing role, the notion of nursing patients with very varied mental conditions within the confines of a ward was actually implausible. In a staff nurse's view:

'It's difficult to cope with the 'knock on' effects of people self harming. It disturbs and distresses others, some of them end up leaving because they can't cope while the self harmers are still here. I'm not attributing blame on them. I just don't think that this is the right environment that's all. One of the girls has only

recently started cutting, sometimes it's quite deep. You're try-
ing to deal with that and at the same time there are another 30
patients on the ward all crying out for attention.'

Another staff nurse opined that:

'The patient mix is bad. You've got chronically depressed pa-
tients mixed with psychotic patients. It doesn't work and they
irritate each other. Not having patients with borderline person-
ality disorder on the ward would help. Trying to manage them
and people on detox and keep the ward safe means that there's no
time for people with mental illness like psychosis, there's no
time to do therapeutic work.'

The overall sense is that therapy, when it occurs, if it occurs at
all, is a hit and miss affair because it operates at the mercy of
events most of which are beyond the control of the nursing
staff. Quite apart from the prejudice that some nurses expressed about doing therapeutic work at all, when it was at-
tempted it had to compete with the coruscating effects of a demanding patient mix resulting in disruptive behaviours,
which, given the conditions, were hardly conducive to good
nursing care. A vicious circle of competing demands between
the (necessary) routines that attend overseeing people in confined spaces, and the desperate needs of psychologically disturbed people, resulted in a matrix of nursing reactions rang-
ing from resigned acceptance to emotional conflict, to
resentment, to best efforts to fight against it. The geography of
the wards also militates against positive interactions with patients: given the tendency of qualified nurses to congregate in
the ward office [ward refuge?] this led to an 'out of bounds'
ambience, a kind of 'them and us' mentality that prevented
constructive, upbeat, interactions.

On the other hand, who could be therapeutic for work
shifts that last for up to eight hours? All other psychiatric disciplines interact with patients for short bursts, rarely extending beyond an hour. If their interactions are longer than this
they will still be time limited, their purpose invariably remaining psychological in nature. For example, a psychologist
working on a desensitisation programme with a patient

would hardly be called away to deal with another patient who can't find his money. A doctor reviewing a patient's medicine is not going to concern himself with the needs of visiting relatives. It has become the lot of the nurses to try to manage practically all the affairs of patients. Even where outside agencies are utilised, such as social work departments or the citizen's advice bureaux, it is the nurses who act as go-between or overseer of whatever transactions are involved. Understandably, perhaps, the ward offices were seen as 'time out' rooms by nurses sorely tried by the multifarious and relentless business of dealing with these 'problems in living' issues. We will discuss some solutions to this in the final chapter. For the moment, it becomes easy to see how the all-encompassing responsibilities of ward-based nurses works against them adopting much more than a cursory therapeutic role.

Chapter 5
What nurses do

*I*n view of the lack of planned nurse patient interactions described in *Chapter 4*, this might be described as the 'so what do nurses actually do?' chapter. As the following examples show, nurses undertake a multitude of tasks that, while not addressing patients' mental health needs directly, contribute to the overall delivery of care and maintenance of the ward environment. It was frequently observed that completing tasks successfully was often undermined by the depth and complexity of demands faced by the nurses. Some of this 'chaos' resulted from the natural busyness of the wards, the inability to predict or control this, and the constantly changing workforce across shifts. The interviews provided some understanding of what the nurses felt about this, as well as what they thought they ought to be doing. Evidently, some nurses experienced dissonance between what they perceived to be their 'desired' as opposed to their actual role.

Routines

What follows is a brief description of the routines and housekeeping tasks that nurses most frequently undertook. Noticeably, qualified nurses undertook these tasks less frequently than unqualified, but they were usually responsible for delegating and supervising them. These tasks included activities, such as carrying out observations, organising and serving meals, medication rounds and writing daily reports. Other activities involved dealing with patients' non-clinical needs; getting to the shops, making drinks, sorting out clothes and money, as well as jobs relating to the smooth running of the ward, such as ordering stores or requesting repairs. There was a ward round most mornings and afternoons where each patient's status was briefly reviewed. Mealtimes were at twelve-thirty, during which qualified nurses departed to the ward office to write up their notes. This was followed by a handover where one shift formally reviewed each patient's progress before handing over to the next shift. In effect, for the duration of the handover, the nurses were unavailable to the patients.

Co-ordination

A large amount of time was taken up with co-ordinating tasks that, despite the usual allocation of a 'nurse in charge' or 'shift co-ordinator', were normally undertaken by several qualified nurses from their 'base' in the office. Communication and the retrieval of information were predominant issues as part of the endless stream of phone calls, coupled with the persistent queries at the office door from patients, relatives, and other professionals. Although not engaged in direct patient contact, nurses discussed patients at length, either informally in handover, or in multi-disciplinary team meetings. They planned care and developed care programmes, but inside a system where the actual interactions with patients were carried out by the nursing auxiliaries. This was also made possible by the non involvement of the auxiliaries in care planning or writing up notes.

> The charge nurse is transferring a patient to another ward. A staff nurse is doing a care plan on the computer and the ward manager is writing a report for a tribunal. The front door needs opening frequently and the ward manager comments that, due to the endless distractions (doors opening and phones ringing), she is 'writing this report one word at a time.' All the qualified staff are in the ward office. There is a ward round in progress and there are 30 patients to be reviewed. Within an hour, five patients present themselves at the office door; one patient who self-harms asks to see a nurse, but is advised that a staff nurse will see her later as agreed. One patient asks to go out for an hour and the nurse has to check nursing and medical notes before phoning a doctor to check the patient's legal status. The patient is sent away twice before this is sorted out. Another patient is waiting for medication to arrive so

that he can go on leave and he repeatedly comes back to the office, as a relative has come to collect him and he needs the medicine now. Two phone calls later and finally a nursing assistant is sent to the pharmacy to pick it up.

During a typical handover, one nurse hands over everyone: that is, she provides a summary of each patient's status to the incoming shift. The information given is often not substantiated and frequently delivered in an offhand way. For example, the nurse comments on one patient who had asked for medication thus: 'he didn't look like he needed it.'

Generally, the sense is of a system in a constant state of flux: the overall intentions may be good, but the sheer disorganisation of the ward—more precisely the way in which events interrupt any attempts at planned interventions or policies—has resulted in systems that are difficult to control. In our view, the very notion of 30 disturbed and disturbing people being nursed in the same place—any place—at the same time is hardly going to facilitate the sorts of conditions where therapy or positive improvements might flourish. To keep these systems operating, outsiders—agency and bank nurses—are frequently brought in. One outcome of this is that, if a patient asks about something, nurses might not know because if they were a bank or agency nurse they would not know the patients. Another outcome is the loss of significant amounts of information about patients. Because not passed on—perhaps because not seen as important—endless time was spent trying to track information down. The situation was made worse when the nature of information being circulated was inaccurate or inadequate in the first place. But, above all, it was the sheer haphazardness of the work that made meaningful communications difficult and often impossible. This was hardly helped by the attitude of some of the doctors who apparently believed that the nurses were there to solve problems for them.

On one occasion, while sitting in a lounge, a staff nurse came to sit with the patients. Within ten minutes she was called back to the office to deal with a phone all.

On other occasions, when staff sit at tables with the patients, they still have to leave frequently to answer telephones or to see to visitors or visiting doctors.

On a particular morning when a consultant arrives for a ward round, a staff nurse is sorting out prescription cards. The ward round starts and the staff nurse, in the office, takes three calls for the consultant from members of the community mental health team. One nurse is sent to the pharmacy to collect a prescription card, which is needed for the ward round. The consultant, at one point, reprimands a staff nurse for not getting him out of the ward round for one of the phone calls. The staff nurse comments that the previous week, he had been reprimanded for disturbing the ward round with news of just such a phone call.

One evening a doctor arrives after dinner. The charge nurse has a list of things she wants him to deal with and spends the next hour (with him) intermittently sorting these things out. The doctor wants to send a fax but cannot get the machine to work. He tells the charge nurse who explains what he needs to do. The doctor still can't get the fax to work and tells the charge nurse who then sets it up for him. He makes a call to see if it has been received and when it hasn't he goes back to the charge nurse telling her it still hasn't worked: his expectation seems to be that the nurse is there to solve this problem for him.

A consultant arrives to see a patient who is not on the ward. The consultant is insistent that he has arranged to come and see this patient. The charge nurse has to make several calls to establish whether the patient is on another ward. The doctor remains annoyed even though it is nothing to do with charge nurse who, in fact, eventually sorts the problem out for him.

These examples illustrate the difficulties of even trying to get out of the office for appreciable periods of time. Because of their pivotal role in 'running the ward', the nurses were expected to deal with almost any situation that might arise. Often, they had to act as temporary secretaries for some of the doctors or other members of the multi-disciplinary team and were clearly seen by them as ward functionaries whose responsibility it was to ensure the actual progress of all events on the ward. The situation recalled David Towell's (1975) description of the psychiatric nurse as 'an intermediary', a kind of 'jack of all trades', steeped in the trivia of ward housekeeping and seeming to have 'opted out' of the therapeutic care of individual patients except at times of crisis, or when the pressure of ward management eased, thus freeing some space for personal contact.

The question of discharge

Nurses were often observed trying to find a consensus about the best approaches and plans for their patient's welfare. In some instances, where the nurses felt that someone should be discharged, lengthy and involved negotiations with doctors and other professionals would take place with this end in view.

A couple of staff nurses discuss a patient who is asking to discharge himself. They include both objective and subjective assessments in their discussion; for instance, a consideration of recent behaviours, including an overdose, which she took at the weekend and the continued risk that she represents. At the same time, they weigh up their personal knowledge of her and their belief that, despite the risks, 'on paper', she is unlikely to kill herself and so should be allowed to go. Their view is that her continued hospitalisation is just making her worse, especially when there are other patients on the ward who are also self-harming.

In fact, most of the nurses think she should be discharged. In the office, her allocated nurse has been trying to get hold of her social worker to organise somewhere for her to stay. She has also been talking to the doctors about her recent disruptive behaviours on the ward as well as, in her view, the inappropriateness of hospitalisation. The nurse has also talked to her friend on the phone who says she is very worried about her going home. The nurse, nevertheless, explains why hospital is not the right place for her. Both the nurse and doctor see her and the doctor insists that she stay in hospital over the weekend at least. The nurses are very angry about this decision and feel that she will become even more disruptive over the weekend when the ward will be less structured than usual.

Busyness

The nurses often had to deal with a multitude of tasks, seemingly unable to complete one task before another presented itself. At different times, they had to juggle multiple jobs to such an extent that it led to cycles of pointless activity, resulting in continued disorganisation and confusion. In particular, several instances were observed where different nurses became involved with issues unaware that other nurses were already involved.

On this morning the nurses are busy and preoccupied. The phone rings repeatedly; there are queries from the community mental health team, people looking for doctors and relatives asking for feedback about patients. Amid all this, a ward round is going on. One nurse sorts out discharge medication while another accompanies a patient to see his doctor. A student nurse is complaining that there is no one about, which means that they have been left (again) to man the phones.

On another morning, the nurses say that they feel fraught. One nurse is off sick and the ward is very busy. A staff nurse says he is staying in the office because he 'can't face going out there'. A patient has a manager's hearing at twelve-thirty while a social worker, Mental Health Act administrator and a solicitor come to the ward to chase up reports and ensure that the patient they wish to speak to is around. Two social workers arrive at the same time—one to take a patient out, one for the manager's hearing—when the phone starts to ring: there is only one nurse in the office to try to deal with all three things at once.

This afternoon the hospital receptionist phones to say that a patient has cut himself in the toilet in the corridor. A charge nurse goes to see what needs to be done. The rest of the staff have gone into a handover and this leaves only one (bank) nursing assistant to 'look after' the ward. This is in contrast to the handover where ten people sit in the office and verbally hand the ward over from one shift to the other.

In this next example, the busyness escalates rapidly because the nurse concerned is not in possession of relevant information and while she tries to deal with the task in hand, other tasks pile up.

After handover, a staff nurse is trying to sort everything out in the office. There are several phone calls in quick succession about two patients, one of whom is about to be discharged. The staff nurse doesn't know about either and has to try and garner information from various sources to ascertain what, if anything has been done about the discharge. A second staff nurse is seeing the ward manager while a nursing assistant takes a patient to an appointment in the main hospital. The first staff nurse is on her own in the office trying to find information when two patients come to the door asking for cigarettes and inquiring when their community psychiatric nurse is coming to see them. The staff nurse responds curtly, refusing to deal with either request. Looking flustered, she swears to herself while trying to sort things out: she asks one caller if she can telephone them back and when they seem to be unhappy about that, she becomes even more flustered. A patient comes to the door again and the staff nurse asks her to wait in the lounge. The patient accuses the nurse of being rude, while the second patient still hovers by the door asking for a cigarette. Finally, the ward manager arrives and is able to deal with both phone calls. The staff nurse sits down visibly relieved.

At one point, I introduce myself to the nurses in the office who say that they are too busy to spend any time with me. I suggest I make a coffee and sit and observe things in the office, saying I'm happy to be left to my own devices. Two qualified nurses then proceed to talk to me about the pressures they have been experiencing recently and this conversation lasts two hours.

On another occasion, a senior nurse is talking about feeling frustrated at her inability to get even low-level patient groups going. She complains that the other nurses say that they are too busy. She questioned whether that was really the case or whether they were just not managing their time efficiently. In her view, many nurses perpetuate a culture of 'always being too busy' and that this acts as rationale for avoiding therapeutic engagements with patients either as individuals or in groups.

This is always a debatable point: whether the busyness of wards is an outcome of pressures—actual work overload—or whether there exists an element of dramatising problems that could be more manageable if handled differently. During the observations for this study, it was clear that very real, persistent and complex demands were being experienced by the nursing teams. This is illustrated by these two examples taken from lengthy observations across both early and late shifts.

Various people turn up to attend the ward round throughout the morning. The nursing office doubles as a reception area and waiting room. The nurses have to deal with these people either by ushering them into the ward round or, in the case of relatives, to the lounge. Alternatively, they have to work around them while they wait in the office. Visitors waiting in the office ask the nurses about other patients or engage in informal chat. The ward round is running late and an increasingly disgruntled social worker waits in the office for over an hour. The phone rings persistently, patients come to the office door and, at one point, there is a queue of three patients and one relative seeking attention.

One patient is discharged from the ward round and wants to go immediately. However, her medication isn't organised so a nurse has to deal with this, which involves getting a discharge prescription out of the ward round, faxing it to pharmacy (at a different site) and then waiting for it to be couriered back. The patient keeps asking when she can go and where her medication is. The staff nurse can only chase her medicine up by phone, which results in the patient becoming more frustrated and verbally abusive towards the nurse. The kitchen supplies are late arriving so there is no tea/coffee/milk or sugar. Five patients come to ask for these items on three occasions and various nurses go and check cupboards before confirming (again) that they are bare. Nurses are then dispatched to chase the supplies up while attempts are made to obtain emergency supplies from another ward. Later, during a different shift, a charge nurse is concerned about the physical well-being of a wheelchair bound patient. It takes nearly an hour to track down a doctor and meanwhile the ward fish need feeding and there is no fish food. Later on, three members of staff from another service come to do an assessment on a patient. The staff nurse does not know why this assessment is being done and neither do the staff from the other service. The staff nurse checks the patient's nursing notes, but is none the wiser. In the end the assessment takes place anyway despite no one knowing why it has been requested.

A doctor comes into the office and without checking who I am, asks about several of his patients. He is impatient to get on, but seems unable to start without a nurse. The nurses, meanwhile, have been trying to get hold of a doctor for nearly five hours: now that he is here, he is unhappy that they are not immediately available for him.

A patient has vomited copiously and, apparently, he had a fit last night before being taken to Accident and Emergency (A&E). A student nurse is left to clean the patient up and the ward manager contacts a doctor while trying to establish what happened during the visit to A&E. However, there is nothing in the patient's notes: he had, in fact, been escorted to A&E by an (agency) nursing assistant and they had not returned before the end of the shift. The nursing assistant concerned is called in to inform the doctor what had happened during the fit, but is unable to answer the doctor's questions confidently. The ward manager tries to ring A&E, but is distracted and does not get through. Just then a patient's husband phones to say that his wife has arrived home in a taxi, which she had no money to pay for and which he refuses to pay. He says she has done this before and that he had told the ward not to let her get taxis home or come home without letting him know. He says that he has told the taxi driver to get his fare from the ward. The taxi driver phones looking for his money and is advised that the ward is not liable for the fare. The ward manager is still trying to get hold of A&E to establish what happened and is still on the phone, on hold. A nurse and patient arrive from another ward (what for?) when the taxi driver turns up wanting his fare. The alarms go off in a downstairs ward and two nurses run off in response. The ward manager terminates his phone call without getting the required information from A&E. A staff nurse is dealing with a new transfer but the wrong room has been made ready for the new admission. A nursing assistant is asked to make up the right room but she is also dealing with the A&E patient who has vomited again and who is also disorientated and wandering in the corridor.

In addition to these periods of pandemonium, however, there were periods where the atmosphere became calm; a kind of sleepy aura would prevail when very little would appear to get done. A sort of aimlessness governed the wards during these periods when the nurses seemed to actively avoid doing very much at all. It may be that these sleepy periods—what some nurses referred to as respite periods— compensated for the busier, frantic, interludes where the pressures must have seemed well nigh unbearable.

A staff nurse and a nursing assistant sit in the office for nearly an hour, writing notes, but chatting informally about kids, schools, holidays and so forth. After a while the staff nurse expresses guilt about wasting time but then suggests that after a very busy morning it was nice to have some relaxation time and take refuge in the office for a while.

Sometimes these quiet periods facilitated relaxed interactions between nurses and patients as well as allowing them to complete non-urgent, but nonetheless important administrative work.

The ward seems quiet now. Various staff nurses are in and out of the office, not staying for longer than they need to sort out their immediate tasks. A community psychiatric nurse and a student come to discuss a patient who has been admitted from residential accommodation. The ward manager and a charge nurse are in separate offices having meetings. The community psychiatric nurse is discussing the details of the newly-admitted patient's stay; for example, his sleep pattern, medication compliance and his attendance at a day centre. The community nurse is passing on useful information about the patient's history and background and this is facilitated by the relaxed atmosphere in the office. The phone rings only occasionally and as the afternoon progresses, staff gravitate into the office to discuss the new patient.

What nurses want to do

During the interviews, many of the nurses gave clear indications about what they would rather be doing and spoke about the dissonance they experienced when this clashed with the reality of their role. Most of them seemed to resolve this dissonance by a resigned acceptance of the pragmatic requirements of the job. One of the issues that ran through the study was the nature of patients' illnesses and the way in which different illnesses elicited different responses from the nurses. Almost half of those interviewed indicated a preference for working with psychotic patients compared to less than a tenth who said they preferred working with borderline personality disorder. Interestingly, over a third of the nurses actively disdained borderline personality patients to such an extent that they (often) openly campaigned for their discharge. The following five staff nurses stated:

'I'm most comfortable working with patients who are clearly psychotic, who have a treatable mental illness, where you can see a definite improvement: when you can see improvement it's satisfying.'

'I do tend more towards clients who are genuinely ill compared with some of those who we get who cause aggro, throwing furniture around because they're not getting what they want. I like working with people who will make progress.'

'I like working with people with schizophrenia. I think it's because personally I find them much more interesting. They have such a broad experience. Its challenging hearing things that you have never heard before, you can learn so much from them.'

'I like floridly psychotic clients; it's what brought me into the job. I find it fascinating. Unfortunately, we don't have that many psychotic patients on the ward. Its 'personality disorder city', it's a nightmare it really is. You get loads of social issues not related to mental illness that you have to deal with nonetheless. We are meant to be an acute admissions ward. It does get your morale down when you are dealing predominantly with clients who need input from social services. We end up 'mopping up'. And there are some very skilful personality disorders who manipulate the service.'

'I like working with young people with psychosis, because you can be dynamic, that's why I came into psychiatric nursing. I didn't come into psychiatric nursing to work with personality disorder.'

In the following extracts, some nurses provide examples of better ways of working that they had experienced previously.

'Here, the handover time is much shorter. Before, we had a couple of hours when both shifts were around and it gives you extra time to do things. We had access to a mini bus so we could take people places; the acute wards had much more resources than we do here. You were expected to go on courses and try different things and then disseminate it to the rest of the team. Different team members would do different things. We used the handover period to do training.'

'We should have less paper work and, therefore, more time to see patients. For example, on an early shift, I can be allocated five patients and not get to see any of them with all the phone calls and paperwork you have to deal with. We need a receptionist; we *are endlessly answering the door and dealing with requests and visitors from the other wards.'*

The inception of Project 2000 in the early 1990s had provoked a range of reactions from traditionally trained nurses. One common reaction was to challenge what was perceived as a move towards academic nursing. Some experienced staff nurses expressed concerns that the new nurses had unreal expectations of their role and that Project 2000 style courses did not adequately prepare them for 'the realities' of the job.

'With our patients we often just see the behaviour and we have no real idea of what's going on under the surface. I think you can get to the stage where you are able to predict behaviour a bit more accurately, but you have to see loads of different presentations. The new training doesn't prepare nurses for that. They spend too much time on the theory and when they get to the ward they can't cope. They want to be therapists, but you need a mixture of 'thugs and therapists' to be effective.'

'The new syllabus is very centred on the academic side, so we get clever people who haven't got a clue about nursing. The degree students are even worse. They don't get the same grounding as we did; they've never seen a dead body, stuff like that. The tutors used to be much more linked to the wards as well; they used to come for half a day. I think that too much knowledge takes you away from nursing. They end up thinking too much and they can't do anything.'

'The student nurses don't do much now. When I started we had to do everything. I find it very difficult to identify the skills you learned with words. One of our new staff is very intellectually capable, but she's got to learn how to do the job.'

Much of the dissonance arose from nurses knowing what they should or would like to be doing, but feeling unable to do these things because of the perceived constraints of the ward.

'I try to treat people as friends ideally, although that is difficult professionally, especially as your first contact with someone can be giving them medication. Your role can change dramatically, due to treatment or legal needs.'

'The problem here is that there is no time to explore. We're look-ing for quick solutions. If we had a little bit of knowledge, we could do better assessment. But the bed pressure undermines anything you try to do anyway.'

'I think cognitive behaviour therapy could work here, but I want to do the course first to qualify what I'm doing and to maintain safety for the client and myself. It would be different if there was someone here in practice that could give you sound supervision—if there was a relevant role model, but there isn't so I want the piece of paper. I've worked with difficult clients and looked for/asked for supervision, but it's just not available. There's a lack of support generally. I was allotted a client when I wasn't even on the ward. In the first session she 'put it all out' then she began acting out. People start to point the finger: 'it's your client, what you going to do about it?' I did some dream work with her which was questioned. So you're always sensitive about not doing anything that they can't understand or don't think is appropriate.'

'I know that I'm not doing as much as I could be doing, I'm ca-pable of more, I'm not stretched, but then I'm not as stressed. I'm not pushing myself further at the moment, I don't want to step on people's toes, or annoy people and people like to do what they know.'

'It is very difficult to do therapeutic work in this setting, be-cause there is no continuity and there is too much else going on in the ward. Patients are moved precipitously. You can't do structured work. I have tried, but if you make appointments you can't guarantee that they will be upheld. Now I do one to one work, but I keep it contained to discrete sessions.'

The absence of continuity and the impossibility of structuring patient interventions have been noted. The following observa-tions demonstrate how the adverse conditions of the wards provoked nurses into acting towards patients in distinctly dif-ferent ways. Of course, this is hardly surprising given their multiple views and attitudes. The intense pressure of manag-ing the wards exacerbated the discontinuities of practice, mak-ing structured (or consistent) interventions impossible.

On an early shift a patient tries to leave the ward. A staff nurse is concerned that he has been violent in the past and does not want him to leave. He says that the patient seems distressed and he decides to spend time with him on his own. During the late shift, a nurse doesn't respond when the same patient says he is going to leave. 'I'm not going to stop him and get a smack in the mouth' he says.

It is noticeable how cynical and/or abrasive some of the nurses have become. Their obvious disdain for theory belies an essentially pragmatic approach to their work. In these final examples, the pragmatism (and the cynicism) are clear.

'I don't think you can have a working relationship with patients; you can't be their friend. I usually have a ten minute chat with people, but I can't be doing with this pseudo counselling. It's a waste of time. At the end of the day I just see myself as a 'benign gaoler'.'

'Patients are here because they have to be here, my job is to keep them intact, to liaise with other professionals, write reports and so on. But I'm not a counsellor. I've got no skills and it compromises your relationship with them. I get pissed off with people going off into side rooms with patients for an hour and talking. It puts the other staff in danger, and getting involved with relatives and stuff. I don't do it.'

'Therapeutic intervention doesn't make any difference. No matter how much you play table tennis with someone, if they're out of touch with reality it's a waste of time.'

One student psychiatric nurse commented:

'On my last placement I sometimes wondered what the agenda was and whether it was more geared towards the nursing staff. The notion that they aspire to Rogerian principles is bollocks.'

Another staff nurse commented:

'As nurses we don't provide 'therapies': we don't have the skills; we 'manage' people. I can only listen to people. I don't have the necessary skills to do more and that makes me feel inadequate. As mental nurses we are not trained to do much. And the current nurse training is appalling. It's even worse than mine was.

These are the future nurses and they are just not equipped to do the job; some students are not even appropriate. You should have commonsense to do this job and some of them don't even have that. You don't get the cream of nurses here, there's no competition for jobs so you don't get the best. Higher qualified nurses don't want to apply here because there's no incentive. You'll take anyone so the standard overall drops and the situation is perpetuated.'

In many ways, the attitudes expressed by many of the nurses stemmed as much from frustration with the occupational limitations of their role rather than from any cool appraisal of what their role might actually be: there was a distinct absence of any collective agreement of what the nursing function should be. On occasions, disagreements (for example, on the question of academia and its relevance to practice) could give rise to cynicism and apparent outright rejection of any place for theoretical discussion. Were agreements about role and function to emerge, plainly they could only do so within a framework that lifted from the nurse's shoulders, the heavy responsibility which they carried for the 'housekeeping' of the ward. Although it was always difficult to see how they had acquired their sense of accountability for every aspect of their patients lives, as well as a responsibility to manage the work of other professionals, they clearly had to deal with this in real terms. The problem (which can only become more acute) is that, given the current obsession with evidence-based practice, it becomes more difficult to defend professional activities whose nature is elusive. Some possible ways of approaching this problem will be discussed in *Chapter 9.*

Chapter 6
Contextual factors

Several contextual factors that impacted on nursing practice were observed: these observations were amplified by the interviews that followed. The contextual factors had a generally negative and constraining effect on nursing practice. Their importance in this study is that they comprised the constituents—often intangible—that governed the actual day-to-day processes of the wards concerned. Call these factors institutional or organisational or whatever, they are the outcome of how individuals and groups become part of the whole, but are at its mercy because remaining, somehow, different from it. In some ways, it might be easy to indulge in a blame culture of scapegoating the nurses, of depicting them as the problem: but, as this chapter shows, things are a lot more complicated than that.

Specific factors

Some of these factors were specific to particular wards, but most were applicable across the board. For example, there were marked differences in the ward environments, some wards having moved from the old asylums to purpose built buildings, while others remained in old or transient hospital environments. Staffing numbers also varied, the minimum staff to patient ratio on different days varying from one to four to one to eight patients. Bed occupancy also fluctuated, with two areas routinely responding to pressure (of admissions) by using beds belonging to patients on leave. Catchment population and size of service also varied from small, largely rural, to larger, busier coastal areas and this was reflected in the size of patient populations on different wards. Whereas, some had large numbers of patients with varied cultural and social backgrounds (often with no fixed abode and/or drug and alcohol problems) in others the patient population were predominantly white and middle-class.

The availability and organisation of support resources in the community also varied, with some services having link nurses, as well as access to crisis teams, assertive outreach programmes or generic community mental health teams. Others had more access to specialist services, such as psychology or cognitive behaviour therapy.

General factors

Despite these differences, some factors affected all areas. The impact of legislation and policy change, for instance, or problems with recruitment and retention of staff, affected all wards in fairly equal measure. The impact of team dynamics, both within the nursing teams as well as in multi-disciplinary contexts, were also noticeable in their effects and it is our submission that the observed variance in staff morale was, at least in part, influenced by these contextual factors.

Staffing

The problem of staffing related not only to the numbers of nurses, but also to skill mix, availability of experienced nurses, and the use of bank and agency nurses. The impact of nursing shortages was a common topic of discussion as, indeed, it always has been: for many nurses, the cherished image of 'hard-pressed nurse' dies hard and is frequently predicated on inadequate numbers. From a management standpoint, there appears to be optimum levels of workload commensurate with nursing numbers and what managers seem to do is work within staff ratios sufficient unto the day, while relying on agency nurses when the in-house numbers—for whatever reason—dry up. Partly as a consequence of employing agency nurses, it becomes difficult to work out an accurate balance between skill mix and adequate nursing numbers. Planning care becomes especially problematic and, at times during this project, even accurate and comprehensive identification of patients and their problems became difficult. During the interviews, some of the nurses discussed the pros and cons of working within shift systems, with particular reference to skill mix. One permanent qualified nurse, says:

> 'I've been working for nine consecutive shifts and this is my third long day and I'm also working tomorrow. It should be my weekend off but there are no staff so I've agreed to work Saturday morning as well.'

A charge nurse comments that despite things being better, staffing is 'still a nightmare':

> 'We want to do things and we have the motivation, but we just can't get on with it because we're still short. I haven't worked a normal week, without having to do extra shifts, for ages.'

A qualified nurse comments;

> 'I think there should be more qualified staff and they should reduce the numbers of nursing assistants. Here, I'm often the only qualified nurse on with nursing assistants. Some of them are very good but some aren't and we work with a lot of bank and agency as well. Ultimately, the quality of care we provide is dependent on the quality of nurses.'

Two other staff nurses bemoan poor staffing:

> 'A lot of the team are very inexperienced; they tend to use a lot of medication. I hate that, we have a definite lack of experienced staff, we don't have people who have got any experience of psychotics.'

> 'It would make a difference if we had better staffing; permanent, regular staff who have been here for a while, working as a team rather than just trying to get through the shift. It would free up nurses to be more creative.'

The latter point is fundamental and goes to the heart of a time-worn nursing dilemma—the way in which nurses (unlike other hospital disciplines) become inextricably linked to ' e wardrunning the ward'. There exists an unwritten rule that, in addition to whatever specific therapy nurses might implement, theirs also is the task of housekeeping the ward and its inmates through a series of shifts across the 24 hours. The mere fact of being with patients for eight hour shifts constitutes, on its own, a strong impediment to doing therapy at all: whereas other professionals enter a ward or other treatment area, usually with some objective and time limited interaction in mind, it can be very difficult for ward-based nurses to do this, especially when the collective needs of 'the ward' supervene. Often the busyness of wards referred to these collective crises; for example, the numbers of patients to be managed or the effects of visitors to the wards (who also have to be dealt with). The 'hard pressed nurse' seemed to result from factors over which the nurses had little control; for example, the assumption that their responsibilities extended into areas of non-clinical management or the quite frequent under-resourcing of a personnel-hungry shift system. At the same time, what managerial responsibility they had was, in various important ways, limited. Nurses had little influence over admissions, although they could bring indirect pressure to bear (on the medics) on the question of discharges. Often, this pressure was covert and emotional in nature, for instance, reflecting the dislike that many of the nurses had for particular kinds of patients.

The relative absence of real power might be partly accounted for by an historical preoccupation with 'doing' as opposed to discussion and reflection. Caudill (1958) showed that nurses 'spoke less' when in the company of other disciplines and Davis (1981) demonstrated an 'inadequacy in conversation and a 'reluctance to enter lengthy conversations'. More recently, White (1985) asserted that theoretical or ideological discussion had not been a major preoccupation with psychiatric nurses. While there is abundant evidence that this has now changed—a burgeoning nursing literature for instance—this intellectual vibrancy is least noticeable among ward-based psychiatric nurses. Within these wards, a cycle of theoretical deprivation has operated to resist change, so that when individual nurses seek to implement discussion or development, they are typically hamstrung by ward systems that kill professional debate, partly in order to sustain the status quo of carrying through their medical functions. An inherent element of such functions is the diagnostic medical language governing how the patients ought to be conceptualised, and it can be difficult to question this in settings that constitute the 'home base' of clinical psychiatry. In Morrall's (1998: 5) view:

> 'If psychiatric nurses operating in the community do not possess authentic clinical freedom, then those who work within the various psychiatric institutions are constrained even further. The medical profession continues to dominate nursing, and the domination of mental health nursing by psychiatry results in the former being tied to the social control function of the latter.'

We turn now to the physical structures of these institutions.

Environment

'Acute Problems' (Sainsbury, 1998) spoke about the out-of-date and often inadequate physical environments that typified acute mental health wards. Our observations about the environment relate mostly to the physical structure and layout of the units and how these influence the delivery of care. Something that occurred across all wards was how particular areas within them tended to be colonised either by the nurses or by the patients or, in some instances, both. This (not always) involuntary segregation had an important effect on how and when nurses and patients paths crossed.

In general, the patients tended to congregate in the communal smoking and non-smoking areas to which the nurses had right of entry, a right exercised only sparingly. Although the nurses had right of entry to any area within their respective wards, clearly each unit's ward office was its headquarters and professional gathering point. Consequently, entry into the ward office by patients was always viewed with some suspicion. On occasions, exclusion rights were made obvious and it was quite common to see office door signs that read 'please knock and wait' or 'please do not enter—we are very busy' or even 'staff only'. During periods of handover or other formal exchanges, entry by patients was strictly forbidden and would have been difficult, since the office would be very overcrowded. While the handover proceeded a single nurse (not necessarily qualified) 'managed the ward'.

These findings show that, in some respects, little has changed in the processes of institutional nursing care. In a seminal study, 'Patient Nurse Interaction' (1972), Annie Altschul mapped the different ways in which ward geography determined patterns of nurse/patient interactions, in particular demonstrating how restricted access for patients impinged on the quality of professional interactions. It was Altschul who drew attention to the 'sanctity' of the ward office and its 'off limits' perception for patients. Although arguably the most famous study in psychiatric nursing history, 'Patient Nurse Interaction' would seem to have had a negligible effect. Consistent with other investigations into acute psychiatric care, we too found the physical surroundings of the wards (as well as their lack of amenities) depressing. However, it was the ongoing segregation of nurses and patients, and the consequent limits this placed on meaningful interactions between them that was most noteworthy. For example, some of the wards had quiet, not unpleasant, lounges where patients might find a bit of peace and non smoking areas were also provided. If required, however, these patient spaces could be used for staff business. In one unit the patient's quiet lounge would be commandeered in order to conduct the ward round, an action highly indicative of 'ward priorities' taking precedence over individual need. It seemed of little interest, even as a matter of principle, that respecting patient's areas as their own might be important.

Also of note was that in few wards was there a central area where both nurses and patients could meet. Nurses rarely sat in the patient communal areas where, typically, the only violation of the silence was a lonely television set. It always felt slightly uncomfortable going into these lounges and strangely un-relaxing. The lounges were typically strewn with miscellaneous items (and none had comfortable seating), which suggested that their possibilities as 'time out' or relaxation areas was not being taken seriously. The absence of communality was not lost on the following four staff nurses:

> 'We've lost the role of the asylum, it was like a small village, a community where you ate with the patients, you worked with them in the gardens and greenhouses.'

> 'It would be nice to have some of the resources we used to have, a swimming pool, cricket pitch, bowling green.'

> 'I think we should have more resources on the ward and more pictures and stuff to make the environment more pleasant. I think there is a view of the acute setting that people should be here for the shortest possible time and therefore the environment shouldn't be too homely, but the environment is very influential on a person's mental well being and I think we could make some simple, but effective changes.'

> 'The patients should be made to feel at home and comfortable, but there is no space, nowhere for them to ventilate their feelings. There's no games room, gym, no occupational therapy on the ward. If you talk to patients, they're bored, there's nothing going on and the nurses don't have time to spend with them. What is there for them; they get up, have breakfast, have their medication and that's it really, meals and medication and sleep with smoking and tea/coffee and television in between.'

Team dynamics and support for staff

In respect of team dynamics, our observations naturally focussed upon relations within the nursing team, as well as on questions of leadership and morale. Relationships between nurses and doctors, nurses and managers, and nurses and community staff were also noted. These observations were amplified by feedback obtained from the interviews. A central theme that quickly emerged was the extent to which the nursing staff did not feel supported by either the medical staff or their nurse managers:

On one occasion, the nurses expressed concerns about a patient who had gone absent without official leave. This patient had a forensic history as well as a tendency to become very violent when unwell. It was the view of the nurses that alternative, more secure, accommodation should be found for him. Before leaving the ward, he had become increasingly paranoid and the nurses became frightened that he would either return (to the ward) of his own accord or that the police would pick him up and they would be expected to take him back. The nurses are actively trying to get the support of the responsible consultant as well as their manager so as to make alternative provision for the patient. There are, however, no alternatives—no placement in a secure unit, for instance—and because the patient is legally informal, there are problems with the police holding him in police cells. Tales of his previous behaviour; for example, taking a member of staff hostage, begin to circulate and this generates more anxiety and further discussion about 'what to do' Despite several phone calls to both the manager and the consultant, the nurses are left without a clear plan or any guidance. The general sense is one of 'what will be will be'. In all probability, the patient will simply be returned by the police and the nurses will then have to manage him, probably by resorting to medicine prescribed by junior medical personnel.

It is significant that the nurses rely on others to take key decisions in respect of these types of problems. In truth, they do not possess anything like the legal powers of the medical staff, which is clearly an impediment to their taking some kinds of decisions. In addition, they operate along an internal dynamic that is reflected in the obeisance, which they show to hierarchically entrenched authority. Hence, the references to 'management' and the desire that management sort things out: not infrequently, a sense of disconnectedness with 'management' spilled over into the interviews. According to one staff nurse:

'If you make a suggestion it's worthless unless they've [the managers] made it: they listen but they don't really hear. I go home and sound off to my boyfriend. I shouldn't be off-loading on him. I feel impotent: you can't talk to the manager because nothing is confidential. I can't go anywhere with my troubles

*because I don't trust anyone. There are different rules for differ-
ent people, but there is no-one there to look after us. Wherever
you work there is inevitably a power struggle, but someone
should take responsibility so that it doesn't get out of hand.'*

Another stated:

*'It's important that you trust your colleagues and that you feel
safe. I learned most from the staff at the old hospital, and the old
consultants, who would always ask you about their patients and
listen. They would take notice of what you said; you were
trusted.'*

Several nurses now believed that consultants had become re-
mote and perhaps even more autocratic:

*'Care shouldn't be driven by consultant psychiatrists. It's like
the alpha pack leader deciding what is in the best interests of the
patient. We are subordinate to a service that is over simplified
by the medical model. That's why good nurses leave.'*

Other factors causing the nursing team concern are to do with
the nursing role and, of course, leadership. The call for good
leadership is echoed elsewhere (Sainsbury, 1998), but it has
been a forlorn hope since the time of the Briggs Report (1972),
which ushered in what appeared to be a framework for modern nursing management. However, because it was too
quickly implemented, it developed no further than a system
for the day-to-day overseeing of traditional wards. It contributed little to the development of professional/therapeutic
principles or practice.

In this study, whenever ward managers spoke about their
work, the central theme revolved around management by role
model. Only one manager declared a need for research to
guide him in his job; the majority took pride in a work style
that often involved the abrogation of leadership; for example,
by taking on the roles of nurses lower down the hierarchy of
responsibility. To be fair, this might be unique in a situation
where there is a need for both good personnel management,
but also a willingness to remain clinically relevant. Some of
the manager's views are as follows:

'I know I'm seen as a bit of a maverick, but I think the unit has good prospects if we can get enough staff. I still do what's needed on the ward first regardless of what my wider role's supposed to be about. I cover for the primary nurses and I have to miss a lot of meetings because the ward's too busy but I'm committed to the team. It is a dilemma with this role.'

'We're clinical leaders. I think we've got very strong leadership here—the F grades as well—we deal with all of it; we can give people concrete advice when they need it or put it back to them so they can learn to work it out for themselves. We are all on a learning curve the whole time so you have to tailor things to individuals' needs, tell people what they need to be doing, give them a bit of direction when they need it.'

'I'm trying to learn myself and teach others at the same time. We need a clinical nurse specialist or a nurse consultant to take on some of the responsibility for us. I don't have enough experience in research to start implementing it here.'

'It is frustrating work, but I enjoy being experienced and being able to model to junior staff how to take therapeutic risks and give responsibilities back to the client. I have been in other areas where this doesn't happen, where there is no clinical leadership and no role models and the effects can be catastrophic, because both the patients and the staff are out of control of the situation.'

Lower down the scale

Comments from more junior nurses on the nature of nursing, as well as individual and team morale, were generally at odds with the perceptions of ward managers, which were hardly idealistic, but were more optimistic and progressive than that painted by those lower down the occupational scale. The latter tended to be negative about the general dynamics and processes of the work environment. In one staff nurses' view:

'There is definitely an air of apathy, but that's about survival I think. People don't want to take anything else on. There is a lot *of low morale. There's been unclear and inconsistent management and lots of people have left. Those that are still here come in, do their shift and go home. We tried to get a support group going, but people had a lot of anxieties; they felt threatened and felt that it wasn't a 'safe forum' so it faded. As for clinical supervision, I've had one session, which happened as it had been originally arranged and the rest of the time it's been ad hoc.'*

Three newly qualified nurses stated:

'After I qualified, I came straight to the ward. I was literally thrown in at the deep end. I was supposed to be supernumerary for the first two weeks, but it was just straight in. I had no time to question why I was doing this. Then before Christmas it was bedlam: a nurse was suspended and I was the last D grade left after three months. The rest of the staff had been betting on who would go first. Certain patients were making people leave. I've been left in charge all the time. I feel under pressure most of the time. I feel 'burnt out' all ready. I've never been as stressed: I've gone home crying.'

'I did have the option before I started of going to work in the private sector, but I decided to face my fears and come to the NHS. Now I feel like I have to keep going to take some personal responsibility for myself and my colleagues. The managers rely on you sticking up for each other, like when things are bad you'll still turn up because you don't want to leave them in the shit.'

'A lot of the new staff are scared. They don't feel like they can cope and there's no-one around to reassure them so they end up jumping in with medication so that they feel like they are in control. Often, that just winds things up more.'

Service issues

Several references were made to the political and legislative pressures on mental health services, and their subsequent impact upon nursing practice. These included: the effects of change driven by both local and national agendas, the configuration of services, incentives for staff, for example, pay and professional development opportunities, and the availability of support resources external to the wards.

One charge nurse expressed concern following a meeting that discussed the potential merger of nursing services with social services, and the development of multidisciplinary teams:

> *'My colleague said I came back with an air of despondency, and I told them that I can't divorce myself from what's going on. Others just seem to let it go over their heads and get on with the job day-to-day, just reacting to whatever's thrown at them next. Maybe that's the best way to be, but I worry too much about the future and the legacy of all this for the new nurses.'*

Three other qualified nurses said:

> *'You become very cynical. I should be the fresh faced one, wanting to give people a chance, but its difficult with the pressure on beds and I get frustrated about the inappropriateness of some of the people we get in here. There's too much politics and not enough nursing going on.'*

> *'When I look back to when I was on nights, it ran smoothly, but there's too much politics today and it gets in the way of patient care, the money for resources is just not available.'*

> *'Better pay would make more of an incentive to come to work, that's why they don't retain staff. What incentives are there for you to come to work? We need staff nurses all the time, yet we have good staff nurses who leave and that's a disgrace. Housing might be an incentive, subsidised housing, or more nurses' homes. People go 'up the ladder' if they're good but we need to keep them on the ward.'*

Here, in these extracts, is aired an age-old nursing concern: the problem of how to create an occupational ascendancy, which allows nurses to acquire professional seniority and status, while, at the same time, prevents them 'fleeing' from the day-to-day clinical needs of patients. The history of nursing is fraught with attempts to solve this issue. Currently, for example, the creation of 'Consultant Nurse' posts seeks to enhance clinical standing by declaiming the nursing role in research (evidence-based) terms. Alternatively, and concurrently, the matron role has been resurrected, a development presumably designed to recreate the authoritarianism of the past: although contemporary matrons are commonly referred to as 'modern' matrons, their re-emergence was vigorously championed by forces on the political 'right' who viewed them as a chance to recapture what they saw as more basic nursing care, nursing care as a hands on, practical undertaking requiring discipline and order for its successful implementation.

Appropriateness

An emotive issue for many of the nurses was the appropriateness of the patient mix on the wards. This related to people being admitted who were not believed to have psychiatric problems that could be addressed in the acute inpatient setting. There was a feeling that, once admitted, these kinds of patients would become stuck and that this would lead to bed blocking for others deemed to be more suitable candidates for treatment. The problem relates to patients diagnosed with borderline personality disorder and alcohol and drug dependency problems. The nurses' comments with respect to such patients related to problems involved in taking risks. On one of the wards, for instance, most of the nurses feel that the borderline personality patients dominate the environment and, although a head count revealed that half the ward's patients were suffering from psychotic disorders, the other half were indeed comprised of borderline personality disorders and drug or alcohol problems. The following seven qualified staff give a flavour of the dominant view:

'I don't feel comfortable working with borderline personality disorder. I think that they are misplaced and, therefore, it just 'fuels the fire' because instead of being able to work with them you have to manage their self harm. We've got someone who coped for weeks and weeks at home and now she has come back in and started to self-harm, much worse. I don't think its an

effective way to use resources. We're a safe place to self harm but I find it difficult to accept this.'

'We have a problem with people with personality disorders. Its difficult because people are admitted for 'quick crisis management', but there isn't the time or the resources to help them properly and 'quick crisis' admissions turn into long stays. It doesn't do them any good. It comes down to what would be best for them clinically being up against fear of taking risks.'

'I am cynical about alcoholics, although it's not just my cynicism. This is a bad environment to work with them; they need to be motivated and to have planned how to work through stuff. When they come here they're usually in crisis.'

'I despair of patients that just won't help themselves, people who whinge, who are inadequate, alcoholics, personality disorders. I hate working with them. We can't help them here and we haven't got the after-care to support us. We've got a patient in at the moment, an alcoholic. He's had three admissions and three detoxes in the last three weeks. We have regulars and we don't do anything for any of them.'

'I think working with borderline personality disorder can affect you more personally than professionally. Its like all the rejects of society end up in the acute setting. They should be getting their lives together.'

'It's not a safe environment a lot of the time. I think we should have more control over who is admitted and we should be protected more from people who are pissed and aggressive.'

'We do get a lot of inappropriate admissions, especially out of hours. We have started using crisis care plans so that if someone who is known to us presents out of hours then there is some information on the ward to refer to.'

The aversion for personality disordered people amongst psychiatric nurses is notorious: one might be forgiven for thinking this relates to the disruption some of these patients bring in their wake. However, while partially true, the issue is more to do with the question of what constitutes mental illness: psychiatric nurses can be extremely tolerant of the most aggressive and anarchic behaviour provided the perpetrator is perceived as being mentally ill. When this is not the case, such as when patients are described as having a personality disorder, nurses can become quite negative (even primitive) in their reactions, in the sense of leaving aside any pretence of professionalism and adopting a position more in tune with the worst prejudices of the general population. We discuss this matter fully in *Chapter 9*.

Moving on

Other (related) concerns of the nurses focussed on their inability to move patients on, once they had been assessed or once they were stabilised. This was particularly frustrating as the various teams were fully aware of the backlog of patients who could be admitted and, possibly, helped. In the view of four of the staff nurses:

'There are three patients on the ward with severe personality disorders and staff complain about the inability to get any of them placed. One has been on the ward for more than a year. They also have one patient who has a dual diagnosis (learning disability) who is also waiting for a long-term residential placement.'

'It's difficult sometimes because people do improve, but then there's problems with referring them on and they get stuck.'

'We often get patients in who have had their medication changed by the doctors (they'll take them off their depot injections and put them on olanzapine) and then they deteriorate and end up being re-admitted. Like patient B, he was on Modecate® but they changed him onto an atypical and he's broken down, possibly lost his residential placement and he's been here for ages.'

'I prefer working in acutes, although a lot of our patients are old chronics. They come in because they start breaking down. We get them stable and then we can't get them back out again.

Sometimes they're here so long they start to breakdown again, usually just as we've got somewhere sorted for them!'

These problems are felt deeply, possibly because the nurses have little executive input into decisions to admit or discharge patients. They can, of course, advise—even cajole, but at the end of the day, it is a medical decision as to whether or not someone is admitted or discharged. It might be possible to consider an approach to discharges based on inter-disciplinary discussion and, no doubt, such practices may prevail in some quarters. However, even when they do, where disagreement breaks out it ultimately becomes a medical decision as to what action to take. In many instances, the nurses feel that their knowledge of patients is more comprehensive, more clued in to the meanings and implications of their behaviours. We were constantly reminded of what the real significance was of this or that behaviour on the part of different patients, for instance, that a patient might be 'acting out' from surreptitious motives about wanting to delay his/her discharge. The willingness of some doctors to respond positively to these patient's behaviours (for example, by not discharging them), rather than agree with the nurses' judgement about underlying motives, caused anger and resentment. On occasions, a 'battle of wills' took place between some of the nurses and the apparent intentions of borderline personality patients. The medical intervention, when it came, had something of the flavour of industrial arbitration even if, occasionally the nurses' insistence won the day. What was significant was that two professions proffered different views, with an entitlement to implement decisions invested in one of these professions only, and the other profession trying desperately to operate according to principles and obligations only vaguely defined.

Chapter 7
Training and learning

Some of the interviews focussed on the nurses' experiences of training and learning. From their responses, it became evident that they had embraced a range of means (both formal and experiential) in preparing for practice.

More than half of the 52 nurses interviewed stated that they had not received any formal training to prepare them for working with psychotic patients, and about a quarter commented that their training was hardly relevant to the job at all. Others did compliment their nursing courses, but in terms of what they had gained in practice settings. Indeed, almost all the interviewees identified experience, 'learning on the job', as the most useful preparation for practice and many of them were able to identify either role models or particular experiences from which they felt they had learned.

Course based training—general

The following interview excerpts reflect the concern that many felt about pre-registration training, and its relative absence of skills acquisition in respect of psychosis. These nurses had been asked: **'Have you had any training that has prepared you for working with psychosis?'** The following Project 2000 (recently trained) nurses were dubious:

'Probably not. You do the theory in Project 2000. Too much theory and not enough ward-based experience. I only did an acute placement in the last six months of my training, I felt very unprepared as a newly qualified nurse. The theory we had was pretty basic stuff about what psychosis is, definitions and symptoms. It would have been much more use to be on the ward learning.'

'We did look at psychosis in our training, but mainly I've learned by being in contact with clients. That makes the theoretical learning meaningful. I sailed through my exams, but I didn't feel confident in what I'd learned when it came to practice. I found that I 'lost my grip' in parts of the course: it was disjointed and didn't relate to practice.'

'We had no teaching on mental illness and didn't look at definitions and diagnosis. I suppose this has a positive side because you can be open-minded, but in terms of how we record things then you need to clarify to others what you mean. Like if you say someone is displaying floridly psychotic symptoms then you know what that means. We were never taught about psychosis, we just had one and a half sessions on medication.'

'There wasn't anything in my training, the topics we covered weren't related. We looked at mental illness, but without going into any real depth. Books I read weren't giving me the answers I wanted either so I suppose I learned on the job.'

'We covered the categorisation of mental illness, but it had no relevance to practice. The practice experience that I did have was completely different to how things are here. The student nurses here do much more than we did. On the placements I did there were always three or four other student nurses there and so you never got to do things like admissions.'

Not all of the nurses, of course, had had a Project 2000 style training; some had qualified via the older RMN (Registered Mental Nurse) programmes. In general, nurses tended to rate these older courses more highly, albeit their reasons for this are always bound to be variable and perhaps even suspect. In nursing, and especially in relation to questions about educational preparation, comparisons between the past and the present often give rise to wistful thinking of the 'things were better in my day' type and this can lead to disparaging whatever in contemporary practice is problematic or anxiety provoking. However, the general feeling among those who had done the older style training was that it had better prepared them for working with psychotic patients. Two senior nurses reflected on this:

'My RMN training did deal with psychosis in a broad sense. I had expected to spend months and months dealing with schizophrenia, but we didn't. We covered things like not reinforcing delusions and we talked about the symptoms. I think it's about as good as you can get. I think you need to have a good knowledge about illnesses.'

'Training in a Bin, it's a good apprenticeship in how to have a normal conversation with someone who is mad. Also 'living in'; it's a normalising process for interacting, being with madness.'

The issue of 'living in' is crucial and hardly anyone (in the literature) has commented on the profound demarcation between Project 2000 and the older courses, which 'living in' represents. In contemporary nurse education, student nurses have little or no geographic focus: they travel from distant parts to a university campus or teaching centre and then disperse when their teaching sessions end. Intake numbers are usually so high that it becomes difficult for them to develop a cohesive identity much less any capacity to link the acquisition of theory with the practice arena, which is now separate from their teaching base, as well as geographically widely dispersed and fragmented.

Previously, student nurses entered a world in which their engagements with patients would transcend the strictly professional encounters that occurred at ward level. Almost all the older training schools were sited within mental hospitals and so students acquired a familiarity with mental illness as a lived experience. In many instances, this included occupying sleeping accommodation within shouting distance of the patient's own. The creation of nurse education institutes within the university system removed these kinds of experience. This 'being with madness', as one former student put it, could perhaps lead to a loss of objectivity and perspective: but it also provided a raft of insights into how patients coped with their difficulties, from hour to hour. Although an air of unreality pervaded mental hospital living (sometimes leading to institutionalisation), the integration of theory and practice provided by being close to patients was surely a good and productive thing. One area in which students might still acquire hard practical skills (related to psychosis) is when allocated to teams whose specific remit is to work with psychotic patients. As one nurse pointed out:

> *'The most useful bit of my training that prepared me the most was working with the assertive outreach team. They utilise specialist interventions and 95% of their caseload is made up of schizophrenic patients. They have a broad range of psychotic experiences and you do a lot of learning on the job. '*

Students were well aware that specific programmes of interventions had evolved within psychiatric nursing practice in recent years (programmes, such as psychosocial interventions or the Thorn approach, for example) and which innovations had been shown to have positive results with some groups of psychotic patients. They appreciated the chance to acquire some of these skills, or at least some familiarity with them and what they were about. A recently qualified nurse said:

> *'When I did my placement with a community psychiatric nurse, I learned some ways of working, about how to put aspects of psychosocial interventions into practice. He demonstrated practical research-based interventions in action.'*

Theory practice divide

Traditionally, a central divide within nursing has been the problems associated with trying to achieve a measure of relevance between what is taught in the classroom and what students experience in practical settings. It could be argued that separating the theoretical aspects of nursing and embedding them within university-based courses is hardly conducive to integrating principles with elements drawn from real life. Many nurses, over the years, have expressed concern that nursing might become too academic; a certain disenchantment has surrounded any efforts to turn nursing into a theory-based activity. For many, the introduction of Project 2000 courses represented just such an endeavour and when, in its implementation, it became clear that the practical aspects of nursing were losing out, pressure arose to modify these courses so as to tie them more firmly into the pragmatic concerns of hospital practice.

So, recent changes to the initial Project 2000 programmes have reflected concerns about excessive philosophising, and contemporary courses are currently being revamped so as to resemble more the older, more medically-oriented, courses. Specifically, from about May 2000, modified courses require students to spend considerably more time in clinical areas. Not only would students spend more time 'on the wards', but they would do so, not in multiples of single study days, but as a series of long continuous placements. Unsurprisingly, some of the interviewees were quite supportive of these changes, although others did believe that attempts to marry up the theoretical material with practice was working quite well. These recently qualified staff nurses commented on the changes:

'My training wasn't any good at all. We covered the categorisation of mental illness, but it had no relevance to practice. The practice experience that I did have was completely different to how things are here.'

'I wasn't impressed with my training. We covered as much as we could academically. We did address working with psychosis, but I don't think we did it adequately; we didn't learn any practical ways of helping people.'

'I did Project 2000 and we really didn't have enough time in acutes. The first 18 months [the common foundation programme] was a pile of crap. It was too general based.'

'The new syllabus is very centred on the academic side, so we get clever people who haven't got a clue about nursing. The degree students are even worse. I think that too much knowledge takes you away from nursing. You end up thinking too much and they can't do anything.'

'You do the theory in Project 2000, too much theory and not enough ward-based experience. I only did one acute ward placement in the last six months of my training. I felt very unprepared as a newly qualified nurse.'

'We had some more general lectures that looked at models, the relationship with stress, etc. Then you come onto the wards and you have to try and connect the two, that's what prepares you for qualifying. I did an assignment on schizophrenia. I looked at my care plan and the interventions I was using. Then I did my case study on a patient who was diagnosed as schizophrenic. It was useful to explore and apply stuff on the ward as well as the classroom.'

'We had a tutor who did approaches to psychosis. He looked at alternative approaches and helped us to understand the perspective from the patient, which was very useful.'

Course-based—specific

Thorn programmes, and cognitive-behavioural models generally, have acquired a new ascendancy within psychiatric nursing, and their central role in helping people with schizophrenia to recover (in the community) has been advocated by many. The provision of Thorn courses in particular has aroused great interest (Gamble, 1995), although cost continues to be a prohibitive factor in encouraging a large numbers of students to do these courses. Most of the nurses here commented, somewhat negatively, on the content of the courses they had already undertaken, as well as the actual difficulties of trying to study further.

'I've done a study skills course and I'd like to do the 998 [Teaching and Assessing in Clinical Practice]. *I definitely want to do some more studying, but it has to be relevant and it's difficult finding anything that is specific to the acute inpatient setting.'*

'I did apply for the ENB650 [Diploma in Behavioural Cognitive Psychotherapy], *and I actually got through the interview, but then I couldn't get funding so I couldn't go.'*

'We did a cognitive behaviour therapy module, but it was focussed on bereavement. I haven't done enough on cognitive behaviour therapy for psychosis, but I'm not convinced it would

work unless the client had insight. I do want to get my head around it more. I have used it with clients who have depression and it has been useful.'

Users

The extent to which people who use psychiatric services actually influence practice varies, but among the Trusts which constitute this study, it could fairly be said that user influence on practice is minimal. However, some nurses did mention some well know users/patients, such as Ron Coleman for instance, and complimented their contribution to mental health care. One staff nurse referred to:

'Ron Coleman and Mike Smith, I went on their day seminar and I got the workbook and I read 'Hearing Voices'. I have used the approaches with patients and have found this very useful, accepting their experiences rather than confronting or challenging them.'

At the heart of the 'hearing voices' approach is a reconceptualisation of voice hearing—normally defined in psychiatric parlance as auditory hallucination—in terms of its meaningfulness to those affected, and not simply looking at the occurrence of voices as an indication of mental illness. Perhaps, as a generalisation, this willingness to listen to patients in terms of their being persons with both a past and an anticipated future is what currently separates some nurses from the diagnostic stance of medical psychiatry. For the majority, however, the general aim was to acquire skills that could then be applied to patients' problems very much in the 'medical mode' of possessing a defined knowledge base with patients seen as passive recipients of therapy.

Experiential learning

Various kinds of experiential learning were identified by several of the nurses. Learning from doing was frequently cited as a real preparation for qualified practice, and this also related to the development of confidence in using and combining both formally taught and more intuitive skills. Learning from others occurred through observing role models in practice and 'experiencing' their confidence. It also occurred through obtaining support, guidance and validation, both through formal supervision and through informal discussions. Finally, learning occurred through being with patients themselves.

At the heart of experiential learning is the acquisition of characteristic ways of doing things that are deemed to be good for practice and patient care. This kind of learning probably occurs at different levels of awareness and is not recognised by the formal educational curriculum, which seeks to control learning by objectifying what is to be learned and then measuring whether or not it has been. On balance, learning by doing, or by imitation, has been criticised because that which is learned is possibly skilful, but, from an ethical perspective, it might be skilfully bad. What, via custom and practice, 'works' in ward settings might simply be being passed on uncritically in the absence of a theoretical curriculum that provides for reflection and evaluation. Educationalists argue that, that which is learned should be predetermined—and thus controlled—by a prepared curriculum. It is surely disingenuous to suppose, however, that skills are not embedded within the contexts of their delivery, or that successfully implementing therapies is not something that takes place in a vacuum. *Box* 2 details some of the characteristics that nurses perceived as belonging to positive role models.

Box 2: Characteristics of role models

Positive characteristics	Negative characteristics
Honesty	Interfering
Taking risks	Thinking you know best
Clarity	Controlling
Straight talking	Belittling
Sensitivity	Using power punitively
Calmness	Too theoretical
Consistency	
Fairness	
Being inspirational	
Professionalism	
Using personal skills	
Making an effort	
Being practical	
Being 'hands on'	
Thoughtfulness	
Awareness	
Not taking oneself too seriously	
Being able to juggle and balance	
Being efficient	
Good communication	
Having a 'lucky bag' of skills	
Remaining human	
Generating ideas	
Being organised (apparently effortlessly)	
Taking time to teach	
Being willing to challenge and change	
Having boundaries but being able to be patient centred	
Being able to overcome difficulties	
Always being with patients	
Creativity	
Being interested in others	
Being confident	
Visible skills	
Being approachable	
Charismatic	
Evangelical	
Psychotherapeutic but also grounded	
Having a good knowledge base	
Giving feedback and supervision	
Being able to have healthy argument	

On the job

Several nurses talked of 'learning on the job':

'Since I've qualified it's been so busy. I suppose I have learned a hell of a lot. I wish I had been nurtured as a D grade for my first year. Instead, it feels like its all been crammed in. I needed to be robustly supported. It does mean that you are more confident. The worse bit was getting used to the responsibility and accountability.'

One nurse was quite forthright about this:

'In the old days you were much more involved and you worked with people who were really barking mad, you learn much more that way.'

Another nurse elaborated the point:

'I think the problem with a lot of the new nurses is they can't problem solve, and they lack assertion. I'm not frightened of people complaining because I'm confident in what I'm doing. I know all the 'shop floor' stuff there's to know through experience.'

An older nurse confided:

'I have learned through experience. I did the old style training in a big Victorian bin. The knowledge base wasn't brilliant especially compared with training now. But even so I think it grounded you more. '

This last point reveals a fascinating insight into the relative value of training as opposed to an education. As Ann Bradshaw (2001) insists, we have assumed that nurses want an education that equips them to think analytically and to ask investigative questions. However, there may be equal weight in asserting that some would forego such a 'knowledge base' in exchange for a training that was more practical and 'hands on'. The following statements from qualified nurses certainly bears this out:

'During my training we had lots of teaching and courses, but sitting in lectures doesn't help much. Being thrown in 'the lions

den' does. You need exposure to the psychiatric unit, you need to have the interplay between theory and experience.'

'Most of my skills have been picked up on the job. My nurse training provided the foundation, but my skills as a person made me an expert. The way I learn is if I do something and it goes well then I'll do it again and vice versa, it's trial and error. It's embarrassing to admit, but I think doctors do it too with medication. Trial and error: there is a loose thread of thought and preparation, and the approach you use gets refined over time. My approach now is much more informal and looser. I was more rigid when I started and now I'm much more open to see what happens.'

'I didn't really start to learn until I was qualified and started to work full-time, but that was quite frightening. In London, as a D grade, you might co-ordinate the shift once a week, but here it's much worse. When I was a student nurse I did a three-month placement on acutes and I did learn a bit, but I finished my training feeling I didn't know enough. I didn't have any confidence, even with some of the practical tasks like giving an injection.'

'Sometimes I feel I would like more training to make me feel more confident, like more cognitive behaviour training. It would be useful for future work. I think a lot of the reason I want training is about confidence, but it would also have a practical application. I wouldn't want to purport to being a therapist.'

'I think you learn through making decisions and having to take the consequences of your actions. Although I am more reliant on my own skill now, I still lack confidence to take on more responsibility. Sometimes I ask myself 'how will I do it' and instead of being able to rely on my intuition, I want a rating scale. I think your confidence in your intuition grows with experience.'

Interviewer: *Which clients do you feel most comfortable working with?*

Staff nurse: *People with depression rather than people who are psychotic because you get feedback from the patient. Also, I've had more previous experience of working with depression and,* *therefore, I feel more confident. Working with other clients is coming together more as I get more confident. It's like learning to drive when you first qualified: you're still thinking about when to change gear, the mechanics of it all.*

Another staff nurse stated:

'Throughout my training I did become more self-aware and I think I learned from utilising other people experiences. A lot is down to experience. The world changes and things are very different now to how they were four years ago. I was lucky that I worked with a good team when I first qualified. It boosted my confidence: we took decisions as a team; we shared ideas, even though the environment wasn't ideal. We used to have groups to discuss how to respond to particular clients.'

And another:

'I think I've picked a lot up from others. I still do, watch approaches others use and learn. Lots of people can be an influence, can generate ideas. Shakespeare, Jesus Christ said lots of interesting stuff, Buddha. I wouldn't listen to celebrity. But I do take inspiration from colleagues, from other patients, from other human beings. I still meet people who will step up my growth. I learn by observation and by asking questions.'

Role modelling was highly reckoned by this nurse:

'My ward manager is my role model. She reinforces my own practice; she gives me courage and confidence. She's also quite practical and hands on and has taught me how to trust my instincts. I've watched how she works with acutely psychotic patients; she uses very personal skills.'

'I've learnt most from the other people I've worked with, I wouldn't say there was a particular role model. I think when people are confident about what they're doing you can learn from them. I suppose that comes from their experience as well. Initially, when you qualify, you're much more careful about what you say, then as you get more experience you know what to say more.'

'I suppose I've picked up different things from different people, like staff nurse A. He has a wealth of experience; he's been

around for years. I think you can profit from working with someone like him. He has confidence, and that promotes confidence a 'net of confidence'.'

'I worked with a nurse in another hospital. She was very confident, I can't describe it but there was a way she was, she fitted in with the patients. She was definitely a role model. It is difficult to describe, in certain situations people can say or do something that you wouldn't have thought of, but you can see its helpfulness.'

This last interviewee draws us back to the central problem in learning by doing or via role models, which is the dilemma of how to separate good from bad modelling.

'The ward that I worked on before here. There were both good and bad role models, but I think you can learn as much from both. The charge nurse and one of the staff nurses were great and we could argue about things, but it was healthy. I got different bits off different people. One of the staff nurses is very laid back, she never gets flustered, but she knows everything.'

Self-directed learning

Nurses were asked about self-directed learning (for example reading) and any individual interests which they had developed. Twelve of the 52 interviewed said that they had no time or volition for such learning, with a further six saying they tried, but found it difficult. Other constraints were lack of resources, such as funding for courses and the availability of appropriate literature.

Nearly half of the interviewees (24) were able to identify areas of general interest and a further 12 gave specific examples, either of philosophies or frameworks that they had read about or that they had pursued independently. This often involved them doing things in their own time or funding themselves on workshops or courses. The next quotes, all from qualified nurses, illustrate some of the difficulties nurses cited in self-directed learning:

'I think I've stagnated a bit. My training seems ages ago, and when I first started I didn't really have much time because I was orientating myself to the ward.'

'I used to read about nursing, but now I'm too tired. If I do read then it's to switch off from nursing.'

Interviewer: *Have you read/heard about any interesting research or frameworks that you think are interesting?*

Nurse: *No. Maybe I'm a bit old fashioned but I want to spend time with the patients rather than reading research. I'm the world's worse. I might flick through the Nursing Times. Generally I have to be made to do any studying.*

'I do most of my reading on the ward when it's quiet. You have had enough when you get home, I sometimes think I should make an effort, but generally I don't have enough energy.'

'I pursue lots of different topics in a self-directed way. I've been reading up on psychosis in my own time (what an idiot). I can't concentrate on the ward and there's not often time either.'

'My time outside of work is very precious so I don't put in time outside of working hours: I want to have a social life. I never get time to read on the ward and even when it's quiet its nice to enjoy having a quiet shift and it means you can spend time with the patients. I'd feel guilty if I was sat in the office reading.'

'In reality I haven't got a second to keep updated, where do you find the time? If I'm not here I'm out having a life.'

'We could do with some decent journals to read that are specific to mental health, the Nursing Times isn't enough.'

The last comment accurately reflected the various ward bookcases that we inspected. Although there were exceptions, they tended to consist of a ragbag of policy documents, an occasional copy of the *Nursing Times*, various patient ratings scales and a file on risk assessment. One bookcase did have a book by psychiatric user, Ron Coleman, and another some material from one of the mental health journals. While many nurses were able to identify interests when asked, these were generally quite broad, or if specific, they were discussed in a vague manner. That said, a fair number did express some interest in pursuing further studies. These six statements from qualified nurses reflect this:

'I am interested in counselling, 'talking treatments'. I struggled with medication, initially, although I know that they can work. I think you have to try and work in conjunction with the client. I like Peplau, you can knock something because it's been around for a while, but there's a reason why things stay around.'

'I'm into alternative therapies like aromatherapy, massage, I think even with psychotic patients you can use it to reduce anxiety. There is so much around that is not utilised.'

'I feel I need more formal training in psychopharmacology, dealing with aggression, specialist approaches like counselling and different therapies, specifically grief therapy and anxiety management.'

'I want to do courses an things that are relevant to the patients on the ward, like schizophrenia, because a large percentage are schizophrenics, but it needs to be specific to the ward environment.'

'I was talking to the psychologist. He came to discuss what he does in his voices group and to go through some tools with us. It motivated me to go and find out about it for ourselves.'

'I am interested in stuff around family interventions. If people are going home on leave to their families and they know the best way to deal with their relative who's ill, it can make life much easier.'

The final examples, again from qualified staff nurses, illustrate self-directed learning that had been taken a step further by those concerned and could be seen to be influencing individual and peer practice.

'The counselling course was good for me. I wouldn't mind doing other counselling techniques, like cognitive behaviour therapy. The course opened up an area that I hadn't thought of before and I enjoyed it. On reflection, I can see that I have developed skills from the course and I would like to develop more. I like teaching students, possibly because my mentors weren't particularly

good; for students to be motivated, they need motivated mentors who will give and share knowledge.'

'I use the Internet at home because library access here is difficult and I buy books. It encroaches on my own time, but this isn't a problem so I fit things in. When we first opened here, I downloaded loads of stuff to create the resource files on the ward.'

'I like Phil Barker and I think that some less tangible ideas are very important, like engagement. That term is very important. It is most important that we engage with people at a humane, respectful level. People are amazing, there is so much diversity. I came into nursing because of Peplau. There is a cartoon that sticks in my head of a man in a hole; it was about empathy about being in that hole as well. It's about Sharing isn't it? If you don't have a relationship with someone then you have nothing. How you get these things, empathy all of that, it's an art rather than a science.'

'I am planning to start a module, next year. I have got some underpinning knowledge. I've read loads on cognitive behaviour therapy. It talks mainly about the processes in the books and I need to know the 'how'. My interest in cognitive behaviour therapy started two years ago when I read Aaron Beck's book and I think it's given me a lot of direction.'

Overall, the educational picture lacks coherence and the nurses differed from each other across various dimensions pertaining to learning and doing. Something which united them, understandably perhaps, was a desire to link theory to practice. More precisely, to view unadulterated theory with some suspicion. Ironic really given that nursing had recently become a university-based activity. Although recent reforms have tried to take account of nursing courses that had been perceived as too academic, there remains the rather troubling factor of a percentage of nurses who shun further learning (even reading) altogether, yet continue to work to the satisfaction of their respective nursing administrators. Equally problematic is the larger group who wish to develop further, but who are constrained by financial and manpower restrictions. Perhaps most significant were complaints about the absence of adequate preparation for working with psychotic patients in hospital settings: the Project 2000 scheme, especially, came in for heavy criticism here, even if its recent revisions had brought some improvement. Lastly, there was the remarkable absence of any evidence base in respect of working with psychotic patients outside the perceived efficacy of the medical model and its prescriptive drugs. Having said that, many of the nurses alluded to an intuitive base, which guided their relationships with patients and allowed them to develop a rhetoric of care that does interface well with much nurse-theoretical writing from America (Benner, 1984; Kikuchi *et al*, 1996) and its counterpart in Britain (Morrison, 1991; Barker, 2000). This could not be said to characterise this sample of nurses, since others wished to develop along very different routes, for instance, cognitive behaviour therapy. All in all, we discovered an extremely mixed bag of nurse practitioners, with most of them lacking any clear guidelines for practice—much less an evidence base—and with some even denying the need for any such thing. This topic is addressed more fully in the next chapter.

Chapter 8
Interventions and approaches

W hen nurses were asked how they worked with psychotic patients, they provided accounts that ranged from the formal (those influenced by a specific framework) to unique and idiosyncratic approaches developed through experience and the working out of individual philosophies. Some respondents used a combination of approaches incorporating formal and informal elements, but generally, it seemed that much of the work with patients was governed by an intimate understanding of their experiences and backgrounds. Although medication was frequently cited as an intervention for acutely disturbed behaviour, its general use was perceived in different ways, some nurses seeing it as necessary and valuable, while others felt compromised and uncomfortable by what they saw as its overuse. The imposition of physical restraints and the use of containment were also mentioned as 'therapeutic' approaches, but these seemed to evoke similar ethical concerns to those described in the use of medication.

Division

The feature that most differentiated nurses across all the wards (into two even groups) was that some subscribed to a known framework as a basis for their interventions, while others appeared to rely on a combination of intuition and long-term experience. About a quarter of those who subscribed to a specific framework were unable to describe what this was, other than in very broad terms, such as 'counselling' or 'risk assessment and management'. Another ten percent claimed to implement more specific frameworks and philosophies, such as 'cognitive behavioural therapy', 'transactional analysis' or 'psychosocial interventions'. A further 15% identified themselves with the use of medication, restraint and 'implementing the Mental Health Act'. The other half of the nursing complement claimed not to be influenced by any model or framework at all, stating instead that their work was governed by 'individual factors'.

This division was also reflected in the way that the two groups talked about psychosis. Some of this discussion was clearly influenced by a knowledge base and framework orientation to psychosis, whereas the talk of those claiming to work without a framework had, at times, a layman's quality about it.

What seems extraordinary is the extent to which large numbers of psychiatric nurses can still feel comfortable—and apparently be as successful in their jobs as their colleagues—in approaching things in an essentially untheoretical way. Over the long occupational haul, it may be that nurses with a more theoretical bent will acquire greater responsibility. However, unlike other professions, nursing has never linked professional progression to academic prowess or the possession of higher diplomas. True, sub-units within the discipline do require formal academic training, for example, the practice of cognitive behaviour therapy usually requires a relevant qualification in that field. That said, many community psychiatric nurses carry out cognitive work with clients without having had any formal training at all. Indeed, one of the few things that community psychiatric nurses have in common with ward-based nurses is that neither group is (necessarily) specifically prepared for their role.

Influenced by a framework—specific

The following examples from qualified nurses describe approaches that were influenced by a specific model, theory or framework. The impetus and evidence for the efficacy of these kinds of interventions appeared to be have been initially generated by external factors, such as reading, taking courses and being involved in research and policy.

'I find Transactional Analysis a useful framework to use. Some nurses do very well with the caring parental role, but I find this difficult as I would prefer to interact on an adult basis. Clients do need or like certain approaches so, if the most appropriate role was parental, I would adjust accordingly. People who are psychotic usually exhibit their free or adapted child. Their adult side is their control, so you need to help them reinstate their adult and to do that you have to be flexible.'

'I like cognitive behaviour therapy because you can give people concrete tangible, constructive ways of dealing with their problems. I find it different to psychotherapeutic ways of working because, often, you can see things and interpret what's going on for a person but they can't always keep up.'

'Having quantifiable skills though is still something that I struggle with. But having had the opportunity to see the principles behind cognitive behaviour therapy working in practice, I accept there is a place for it. I think you can confront the delusional belief system, you can de-catastrophise what people are thinking and normalise their experiences. I like the psycho-educational stuff. I think people with serious and enduring mental illness are often forgotten and left without active intervention.'

'I think education about medication is very important for compliance and that's the major thing in the long term. This Trust is very medical model orientated. But medication is only going to work in the long term with education. I'm doing the psychosocial module at the moment and the other important aspect is about working with the family.'

'I did a case study on schizophrenia, and through that I picked up a lot about accepting the person's reality, being tactful about accepting their reality. Bentall wrote a book called Reconstructing Schizophrenia. It talks about a continuum of psychotic experiences; schizophrenia doesn't necessarily exist, it is much more about individual experiences of people.'

The medical background (or model) is something that all ward-based nurses must grapple with and we found little evidence of collective resentment to it, albeit some were sceptical about the extent to which physical treatments, especially drugs, permeated the atmosphere of the wards. Interestingly, most of those espousing a particular framework had named psychosocial interventions and cognitive behavioural therapy (which are linked), the two approaches that most resemble the medical model. This is in the sense of their being oriented towards a prescriptive, therapist-led style of interacting based upon ideas alleged to be grounded in empirical science. However, although these cognitive approaches were popular with some of the nurses, they did not affect the general tenor of the different wards' activities, which proceeded along a fairly pragmatic route of managing the ward and attempting to keep it calm and conducive to the general recovery of its patients: it is this lack of specificity that allows an array of nursing actions to proceed pretty much in the absence of any framework or pre-determined schemes of interventions. In her ground-breaking study, Altschul (1972), too, noted an absence of theoretical or other frameworks by which nurses were guided in their work, although she did not see this as any great defect. Whatever the implications might be, it would appear that, in some respects, little has changed in 30 years.

Influenced by a framework—general

Some nurses appeared to be influenced by more generic frameworks drawn broadly from social, psychological and medical models. Many of the following examples, however, reflect free-floating approaches grounded in intuition and experience.

From a staff nurse

'The relationship you have with your clients is central; you can have all the theoretical background in the world, but it's meaningless if you don't have that relationship. I think you can always apply basic Rogerian and Peplau approaches, but it can be difficult with people with psychosis who have so many different layers to unravel.'

Interviewer: *When a client is admitted who is described as psychotic, what do you find is most useful in terms of how you approach/work with them?*

Staff nurse: *Patience, listening to them, and being very observant. If someone is already described as psychotic, you still need to be aware and objective, try and establish if there are any elements of truth, really listen to what they are saying. At the same time you have to ensure safety and preserve their dignity.*

Interviewer: *In your experience what approaches do you think are most useful when working with someone who is described as psychotic?*

Ward sister: *Look at previous interventions to establish what works and what doesn't. Find out if the psychosis is distressing and ask the patient: 'what helps you?' I wouldn't automatically resort to medication. I would try and use distraction instead, try and give the person some control back. Try to find out what triggers the distress; are they reality-based at all; often there is something there you can work with. Once they're stable, I think there is a place for education, recognising symptoms, giving back control, providing information about available resources, helping them to identify strategies to prevent relapse.*

To the same question four other staff nurses responded thus:

'The environment, making the environment calming, make him feel safe. If you don't make him feel safe, you will have a problem; that is, he will abscond or he will become unmanageable.'

'I try to make them feel as safe as possible in the environment and around others. I start to try and make a relationship; unless there were obvious issues, like safety that needed addressing, I would be fairly low key.'

'When someone is admitted, I look at their history, although with an open mind. I try to go through the assessment process and identify presenting problems. It does help if you've got previous knowledge, the main thing is to do a risk assessment, and again the history is useful.'

'Your interaction should be clear, brief and short, trying not to get too involved in their delusions and beliefs. Try to reduce stimulus and avoid arousal; if they're not up to interaction then observe them discreetly. If they're suspicious or paranoid, you can make it worse by asking too many questions. The importance of observation was stressed in my training. You don't want your first interaction with a psychotic person to be unpleasant for them.'

While these responses stem from the well of experience and not theoretical analysis, it may be that they have acquired a level of validation by constant cross matching with similar responses from others. Indeed, the nature and style of many of the comments suggested a sort of 'agreement in kind', which operates on the wards, pertaining to a wealth of received ideas about what practically works with psychotic clients and what doesn't. Time and again, nurses made references to the need for good observation (a sound scientific principle), as well as the need for pleasant surroundings and an absence of stimulation. Again, while seemingly derived from a mixture of intuition and experience, the desire to provide a kind of neutral setting for psychotic patients does find resonance in empirical research, such as the finding that schizophrenic recovery is significantly improved when patients are not subject to high levels of emotion and, especially, critical judgement (Leff *et al*, 1982). So that what appears to be, at first inspection, groups of nurses working outside any framework or empirical tradition is not quite accurate: nurses appear to acquire methods and skills that do not, in fact, always run counter to what has been established via research. The issue seems to be the extent to which they articulate their actions in abstract terms. This is also nothing new and psychiatric nurses have, from time immemorial, found difficulty in delineating their work in abstract terms; in some cases finding it difficult to discuss their work at all.

Medication and the Mental Health Act

Medication was described both positively and negatively; some called it a 'necessary evil' believing that it was an effective means of alleviating distress. It was also viewed as an expedient means of dealing with people's behaviour in the absence of other options. Nurses from one ward seemed to rely more heavily on medication and other physical interventions, although they acknowledged this and tried to explain it as due to poor staffing and the unavailability of experienced nurses. The following quotes demonstrate the dissonance expressed about the use of medication and other physical interventions and the extenuating circumstances that lead to their implementation:

> *'Basically you are co-ordinating care, and administering medication. It's about maintaining safety; you don't do any one-to-one work. Anything other than medication comes from other disciplines. In the acute setting, people are acutely psychotic. You can't engage in work with them until they're stabilised. By that time they're being moved on anyway.'*

Another nurse was asked: *When a client is admitted who is described as psychotic, what do you find most useful, in terms of how you approach them?*

Staff nurse: *Medication first. You have to think about safety and not just about the person, but about the state of the ward. You can't really interact with someone because of the environment. You should be able to but we can't really, here.*

Another staff nurse stated:

> *'I am interested in medication in relation to psychosis. It may not be the most dynamic approach, but it is very important. There are two extremes in the use of medication; they can be overused, but they can be underused as well—people are much more aware of the former. We encourage clients to be independent and autonomous, but while they're here, they can't self medicate; the nurses have control and that creates all sorts of issues about power, etc. If someone asks for medication, I sometimes feel embarrassed that I have to be in that position of control in*

the first place, but I will give the medication. I feel very uncomfortable about denying them control over how they feel and how they manage that. I think it's a strange and hypocritical situation: if they were an outpatient, they would be given benzos [benzodiazepines] to use when they get agitated, but here there is a belief system that everyone taking benzos will potentially abuse this, and maybe it's a fair comment to some extent, but it can also be a way of developing a negative view of the client, that is, if they ask for benzos, its not because they're ill or agitated, but because they like the benzos.'

Another nurse stated:

'Drugs have a very big role, despite the fact that I'm not into the medical model. You use medication because there's not enough time. Ideally, medication should be used in conjunction with other interventions. Basically, medicine isn't time costly. Also patients won't necessarily respond to other approaches.'

The following statements describe an acceptance of the use of medication and more positive views of their therapeutic value. Sometimes nurses considered their use in conjunction with other approaches.

Interviewer: *What approaches do you find most useful when working with someone who is described as psychotic?*

Staff nurse: *Adherence to drugs, whether they like it or not. I make sure that people get their medication, otherwise you are just leaving problems for the next shift. I think Acuphase is the best option, if they are disturbed. It controls their behaviour and treats their psychosis and, if you have to jab them, then its better to give them something that's long lasting.*

A charge nurse responded to the same question:

'It's a balance between knowing how to respond to people, but also being prepared to give them decent treatment if they need it. I'm quite medication-orientated, especially in the early stages. Often, when people are admitted, they have already been assessed and medication has been prescribed. If assessment is still ongoing, then no medication may be appropriate, but I still

see the priority as getting them assessed and getting them medi-cated as soon as possible, otherwise it can be a long haul.'

Individual factors

These types of intervention were characterised by their unique and idiosyncratic nature, either in the thinking behind the approaches used or the creative and innovative things that nurses did when engaging with patients. We found much evidence that nurses had developed an individual and intimate understandings of the patients they cared for, and some claimed a particularly good understanding of psychosis and its meaning. The following descriptions—all from qualified nurses—highlight personal understandings of individuals and of how they experience psychosis.

'People with psychosis have so many different layers to unravel. They can change daily; sometimes they can't contain it, but usually, there's a lot going on under the surface and you can miss an awful lot. Because they can be suspicious, have poor concentration, have no reasonable or consistent conversation, it would be reasonable to say, 'I'm not going to get any sense here' and not bother spending time with them. But you need to listen. I think nurses either tend towards psychotic clients or not.'

'When patients suffer with psychosis, I think it's very real and genuine. I feel I can relate to the clients and I have more patience. I enjoy the variation in their moods and presentations. With patient B, it's about her expressed needs, not nursing needs. Its not really about schizophrenia, its about her, she feels she has lost her identity and she'll cry because she can't make her own mind up. She has all these insecurities and paranoia about being sent away. It's so rewarding empowering her to make choices. I'm not kidding myself about what I can achieve or that it's always rosy. Sometimes she tries to control things by pushing boundaries and testing out whether I care. She can be horrible. But she had a really good relationship with the manager in the residential home where she was and when that

placement ended, she felt very insecure. Now she's constantly questioning her future.'

'There's a school of thought that you shouldn't talk to patients about their psychosis, but that's like someone having a bad foot and you refusing to talk about their foot. I think it's important to give lots of reassurance, give information about what's happening to them and try to create safety for them in the context of their experiences, explore what their fears are.'

'I would describe psychosis as the disjunction between the subjective perception of the patient and the loosely knitted consensus of the world view of the observers. It shifts with the political climate. It has to be causing some form of distress or risk to the self or others to come to the notice of professionals. Other agendas come into this, like the desire of medics to treat symptoms whether it is necessary or not.'

'I think that trying to make sense of psychotic experiences when someone is well again can be difficult, but often it is possible to explore experiences and understand them retrospectively. I suppose this happens when they go back to the community, but there's no reason why it couldn't happen in the acute setting. With permanent psychosis, drugs suppress the ability to explore these experiences.'

'During my training, we looked at the diagnostic criteria, but it never really sat comfortably with me. If someone has a diagnosis of paranoid schizophrenia, and they are apparently distressed, you can tell them that they're safe without denying what they're experiencing. I think psychosis has dangerous associations with the mad/bad notion. People with a diagnosis of psychosis often struggle in the wider community outside of mental health services, where there is stigma and value judgements made about what it is. Sometimes I read nursing or medical reports and you'll come across 'experiencing auditory/visual hallucinations' and I wonder if people reading or writing that put their own interpretation on what it means without understanding what it means to the person. There is so much labelling, it doesn't allow for different cultural factors. Visions can be an accepted part of someone's spiritual culture, but they could

also be interpreted as illness by psychiatrists. Most medics come from the same cultural and socio-economic background, which perpetuates the dominant cultural norms. I think that probably psychosis becomes identifiable when it starts to trouble others and not necessarily the person themselves.'

Another nurse opined that:

'Psychosis is individual to people; you can quote all the text book stuff, but it still comes down to the person. Sometimes it can be very subtle, it can be very difficult to know what someone is experiencing unless you know them very well. A lot of it is down to interpretation as well; someone who says he is Jesus Christ is likely to get themselves sectioned, but it could be true. Sometimes people have very plausible stories—like the patient on the ward at the moment—when he was admitted he was going on about his neighbours being drug pushers, it was very convincing, but we didn't check it out. We just assume that it's not true. Often there is some basis in truth, but it just gets blown out of proportion. We don't explore it enough, find out what's caused it. It's too easy to just give drugs.'

Four other staff nurses give their views:

'We know the patients so well here; you get to know their per-sonalities, what they will react to and what to avoid with them. Like patient A, he makes requests specifically to me, when he hasn't made any contact with other staff. He's a bit like a time bomb when he's trying to hold it all in, he can't control his frus-tration. I can feel his suppressed anger, I can sense it; if you say the wrong thing he can blow. You know their patterns, it comes with experience, with familiarity.'

'With someone who's psychotic, you've got to consider all as-pects when assessing their needs; for example, one patient had particular beliefs about food and therefore he had to eat before every one else. You need to assess his dietary patterns to pick that up; then you need to understand his thinking to help him to find ways of coping and making sure he gets fed. There's the human element in it all no matter how many books you read. Sometimes you have to rely on your life skills; if you're too clini-cal or controlling, patients won't come to you.'

'I try to talk to patients about their experiences, not in a confronting way, but trying to gather information, to try and develop an understanding of their perception of their experience and their primary needs (rather than relying on my own perception of what their need is). So, for example, if a patient is saying that they want blankets to protect them from the radiation even though it may be seen as being collusive with their delusion, I would give them blankets if it helped to make them feel safe. I would try to sort out where the belief comes from and what allows them to function with that belief. I try to get a sensible perception of what they are experiencing and how that is making them behave and then, if they need to bath at night or they want to sleep on the floor, because they believe they are being poisoned by gases, its OK. It's not difficult to accommodate bizarre behaviour and ultimately it can help the patient to see that we are on their side.'

'Some patients do respond to me, like patient A who can be very difficult. I don't know why he responds to me so well. I think he appreciates those nurses that give rather than take all the time. It's not a hardship to give people a fag or take them a cup of tea, or take their medication to them. You have to remember that they're human, not just a patient or an illness, common courtesies are important. And people still have a sense of humour; you can have a laugh and a joke. A lot of the younger nurses are frightened of using their humour. I think these days you get told off for being over familiar. You can get reported for putting your arms around a patient. I know we have to have boundaries, but a lot of the old chronics don't understand boundaries and if they like you, despite everything that you might have done to them over the years, that's really important. If you're too over-sensitive about boundaries, you're not going to get a real rapport going. I suppose a lot of it is about knowing yourself and experience so you don't get into difficulties.'

These final examples illustrate the range of individualised interventions that nurses utilise. Some are 'customised' versions of more conventional approaches, but others appear to be unique, innovative or to stem from instinct.

Interviewer: *What do you find the most useful approach when working with someone who is described as psychotic?*

Staff nurse: *A lot of the time you're 'winging it' seeing how they respond and adjusting your approach accordingly. Being honest and genuine, not worrying too much about saying the right or wrong thing and just concentrating on being there for them. Listening and communicating skills are important, people will respond to lots of different things. Being patient, trust and respect will develop gradually. It's about saying I'll meet you half way, I'm here for you, I'm reaching out to you, my hand is there and it will stay there until you're ready to take it.*

One staff nurse was preoccupied with the nature of skills acquisition:

> 'You have intuitive skills that you can't pick apart, they can't be easily described and often they shouldn't be because they are complex in nature. Sometimes the most effective thing is a fag and a cup of tea. Or a familiar face. We had police bringing patients up to the ward and they're supposed to be raving and then they see a familiar face and they calm down. A lot of what I do is creating a calm environment, just calming things down and creating the right 'milieu', intervening with problems as they erupt and soaking up the inexperienced staff's worries.'

In one sister's view:

> 'You have a different rapport with someone who is a chronic schizophrenic. They're not really on this planet, so you have to try lots of different methods to try and get into their world. A sense of humour helps. If they don't like being formally assessed, you can still find things out indirectly, using more subtle means. Just gently pick away at the surface. Like patient B: I've known him for years. I butter him up with my personality; you can get away with it when you know them well, have a laugh, be a bit more relaxed. It comes with experience. You need to develop a good relationship, keep gently approaching them, because it pays in the end. If they come back, it doesn't matter how psychotic they are, they still remember you and you can use that.'

A staff nurse believed that:

> 'You can have an instinct about patients. I kept on approaching a particular patient because I didn't think things were right for her. I tried to give her options. I used my personal experience, common frames of reference (we're both from Mauritius) to start some rapport and then asked her a bit more about her feelings, asked her to be honest.'

Another nurse, when asked what was most useful for working with psychotic patients, replied:

> 'Get them to relax, no pressure, don't restrict them too much, show them their room, be gentle reassure them, tell them things again if they're not taking it in, reassure them that they're safe, they're not on their own. Say that things may feel bizarre for them, but they're not bizarre to us, encourage them to go with it and not fight it. It does help if you know the clientele although it can make you blasé as well. You might think you know how they'll be, but they can always surprise you. You shouldn't take them for granted.'

One telling comment came from a staff nurse who confided that interventions with patients were more to do with issues on the day and less a matter of theory.

> 'I always make sure that everything is explained to patients, allay their suspicions. Most nursing skills around admissions are around your intuition. It's difficult to apply a model, so you are guided by the patient's responses and you respond accordingly. I try to make them feel as comfortable as possible. The way that different nurses do it is very individual; they have their own personal model. I believe in a flexible approach, compared with nurses who have a checklist. You have to follow the protocol of the environment you're working in, but again you need to make it work for the individual. If you are working with someone who is floridly psychotic, then the important thing is for us to fit in around him or her. I wouldn't nurse two psychiatric patients the same way because the relationship you have with them is very individual.'

Chapter 9
The professional relationship

*H*ildegard Peplau (1994), a seminal voice in psychiatric nursing, always insisted that 'the nurse/patient interactions with the most potential for therapeutic benefit are regularly scheduled counselling sessions.' The nurse patient relationship is held to be central to the patient's recovery and is the yardstick by which professional nursing should be judged. However, the nature of that relationship has always been in question and many studies have focussed on this (Altschul, 1972; Cormack, 1976; Gijbels and Burnard, 1995; Higgins *et al*, 1999; Towell, 1975; Whittington and McLaughlin, 2000). A consistent finding has been the limited amount of therapeutic time that hospital nurses spend with patients: it is usually given as between 6% to 12% in cited studies. Although direct contact with staff has been identified by patients, as one of the positive aspects of inpatient care (Baker, 2000; Cleary and Edwards, 1999; Pilgrim and Rogers, 1994; Shields *et al*, 1988), it has been shown, time and again, that this occurs with insufficient regularity: this finding is reconfirmed in this study.

The nature of nurse/patient contacts has also been explored. Gijbels and Burnard (1995) examined the suggestion that any interaction could be potentially therapeutic, while Pilgrim and Rogers (1994) noted the value placed by patients on 'ordinary relating, talking, listening and respect'. Cleary and Edwards (1999) found that patients appreciated the nurses' interest, patience, friendliness and 'just being there'. MacGabhann (2000) suggested that patients often had difficulty identifying what nurses actually did to improve their mental health, but were 'sure that they were doing something'. Cormack (1976) found that most nursing time spent with patients was in social conversation; while acknowledging the importance of this, it could hardly be classed as psychotherapeutic. MacGabhann (2000) also thought that 'social conversation' was not enough for patients, and that more emphasis needed to be spent on developing relationships. He found that patients wanted more one-to-one sessions and individual therapy, a view echoed by a recent MIND report (Baker 2000).

Crisis/reactive interaction

Of the 40 interactions we recorded, the majority (29) were defined as crisis or reactive responses precipitated by unforeseen events that potentially created a risk to the affected patient or to others. Other reactive responses related to opportunities created by the nature of the ward at a given time: if the ward was quiet or more staff were available, then this allowed more social or recreational interaction to take place. Sometimes nurses appeared to adopt a 'let's see what happens' approach that could be deemed therapeutic, since it allowed patients to deal with their experiences, at the same time as leaving the way open for any interventions that might be required. In some cases, this avoided using medication or physical restraints unnecessarily, but at others 'wait and see' lapsed into 'doing nothing', with the nurses taking the path of least resistance and offering the minimum interactions possible.

Planned proactive interaction

Planned interactions with patients were rare and indicate the extent to which the nurses' activities were actively curtailed by other pressures and demands. It could be argued, in a context of working with psychotic patients, that therapeutic value could derive as much from unplanned as planned interventions. Even if unplanned, a five-minute interaction with a schizophrenic patient could be as beneficial as a planned one-hour session with an insightful patient. In our view, interactions were dictated largely by external factors and, although the crisis/reactive interventions reflected the diversity of patient's needs, nurses need to develop more control in respect of providing sustained therapeutic interventions with patients.

Getting a response

Disturbed behaviour was likely to get a response and dangerous behaviour always forced a response. Where there was no immediate risk or where the patient was seen to be in control of what they were doing, a policy of deliberately ignoring them would be implemented. Alternatively, patients persistently presenting with 'nuisance' behaviours could not be ignored and nursing responses here were often unfavourable and punitive. The final Report of the Royal College of Psychiatrists (CRU, 2000) suggests that such staff responses are likely to contribute to the genesis of violence. Others (Rose, 2000; Walton, 2000) also describe aggressive staff responses, which lead patients to adopt disruptive behaviours aimed at manufacturing attention. This was especially true where patients were believed to suffer from borderline personality disorder. Disturbed or aggressive behaviours that were assumed to result from illness were dealt with more sensitively and, subsequently, such patients were still perceived positively and their aggression 'excused'. In their paper, 'Chancers, Pets and Poor Wee Souls', May and Kelly (1982) discovered that:

'what is critical in determining nurses' categorisation of some patients as problems is not so much the level or nature of patients' demands, as much previous work has suggested, but rather the patient's willingness to legitimate the nurses' therapeutic aspirations' (p:279).

In May and Kelly's view, psychiatric nursing is unable to call upon readily identifiable psychiatric skills. Its authority is ambiguous and must, therefore, look to relationships with patients as a means of ensuring forms of personal and professional identity. Personality disordered patients reject the ministrations of psychiatric nurses and thus are resented because they scupper notions about good ward management and patient care. May and Kelly observed that part of nurses' positive self-evaluation is a self-perceived ability to cope with demanding patients and situations: the personality disordered patient capsizes this most prized belief. Contrariwise, the disruptive behaviours of psychotic patients are viewed differently because there is a presumption of lack of insight on their part. In other words, these patients are seen to reject the nurses' ministrations because they lack the mental autonomy to do otherwise. More recently Clarke (1996) also found that patients with personality disorders had an aversive effect on many of the nurses and that some reacted angrily at the very presence of these patients in their units.

Desensitised

An interesting twist on this is that some nurses may become desensitised to certain behaviours and so tolerate them despite their negative impact on the ward's atmosphere or other patients. Lepola and Vanhanen (1997), for instance, found that nurses had gradually begun to tolerate what they once regarded as anomalous or difficult behaviour provided it did not result in overt aggression or serious disruption. We also discovered that, for significant stretches of time, nurses became immune to patients who were then left to their own devices, often relying on each other for advice and support. Similar findings have been reported elsewhere (Baker, 2000; Rose, 2000; Walton, 2000).

The lack of interaction could also be seen as enabling nurses to withdraw from potentially stressful environments. The nurses frequently complained of excessive exposure to the traumatic experiences of patients and complained of violence and verbal abuse. Some were needful of adopting avoidance behaviours, distancing themselves both physically and emotionally from patients so as to maintain their own well-being. Isabel Menzies (1960) had argued that the attachment of nurses to ritualist behaviours was precisely to defend themselves against the endless threats that close emotional contact with patients brings. Other (psychiatric) studies, which support the protective role of defence mechanisms, are by Bowles (2000), Walton (2000) and Whittington and McLaughlin (2000). Bray (1999: 303) describes his experience of exposure when doing a participant observation study:

> 'I experienced a feeling of profound cognitive and emotional tiredness as I attempted to work in the way prescribed. The resources I had included time, limited involvement, a good theoretical understanding of my work, but even so I could feel the beginning of an urge to retreat to the office.'

One of the present writers (Clarke, 1996) had explored this issue with various ward teams. In discussions with a psychologist, the latter believed that reading newspapers (and thus blocking out patients) in the communal areas of the ward was simply a means of coping:

> 'The issue is not one of scapegoating or labelling people, lazy, etc, but why they do it. I find that I do it, read the paper: some of the patients you could not easily talk with' (p342).

Some nurses, however, frustrated at their inability to interact with patients in a more relaxed way, were dismayed by the notion that they only seemed to be there to respond to extreme behaviours. The point about not being able to talk to some patients is also important and others spoke of how difficult it is to relate psychotherapeutically to psychotic patients. This, of course, largely depends on what is meant by psychotherapy. In any event, such beliefs are no excuse for not attempting to interrelate with patients at all. Yet non-involvement was almost characteristic of the wards for prolonged periods; a passive ritualism prevailed, which can only be interpreted as a protective mechanism of some kind.

What nurses do

Many years after her original study, Menzies Lyth (1988) further described institutionalised practices and routines utilised by staff as a means of containing their anxieties. Bray (1999) argued that the continued relevance of these in inpatient settings as 'individualised care and the nursing process become task orientated, ritualised and formulaic in practice.' Peplau (1994) acknowledged that 'inpatient psychiatric nursing provides a wide scope of activities, many of which support the safety, well-being and amenities for daily living of patients', but that these were not as significant as interpersonal activities between nurses and patients. Altschul (1997) seemed to recognise a less idealistic world where:

> 'Sharing the patients daily life, wherever that may be, observing and communicating in the course of other activities, piecing together a picture of the patient from fragments of information obtained as a by-product of activities is, in my opinion, every bit as important as individual therapeutic work' (p11).

Perhaps so: these processes ('other activities') become problems when they slip into the routine and humdrum. The relationship between ward routines and nurse/patient contact is frequently mentioned in the literature (Antoniou, 2000; Jones et al, 2000; Mulholland, 2000; Walton, 2000) with the time spent on 'routines' being significantly greater than that spent on 'individual therapy'. These routines range from the broader service activities of 'admission, assessment, stabilisation and discharge' (Godfrey and Wistow, 1997) to more functional routines, such as supervising meals, giving out medication and supporting patients (Whittington and McLaughlin, 2000). In all areas observed during this project, both generic and local routines were common and constituted the general framework within which the ward did its business. Routine, however, is a double-edged sword; for example, qualified nurses usually delegated observation and other routines to nursing auxiliaries and this was in keeping with their self concept of professional status, which stopped them engaging in 'non-nursing' activities. However, paradoxically, this allowed the nursing auxiliaries to interact with patients much more than the qualified staff who would collapse into paperwork and/or administrative obligations.

Barker and Cutcliffe (1999) cited a growing emphasis on observation as a main focus of nursing activity and its detrimental effects on both patients and nurses, negating the development of meaningful and therapeutic engagement. Bowles (2000) argued that 'the preoccupation of mental health services with risk and dangerousness' had led to an increasing focus on routine and controlling practices, such as close observation, and that such practices conflict with parallel demands for evidence-based therapeutic interventions. The report, 'Acute Problems' (Sainsbury, 1998), noted that more than half of their observed patients had undergone some form of observation, with at least a fifth being subject to at least one period of intense, constant supervision. In their extensive review, Barre and Evans (2002) observe that this is a practice that is 'sparsely researched and poorly understood' and they note the conclusion of the Standing Nursing Midwifery Advisory Committee (SNMAC, 1999) that 'little consensus about the principles, practice and procedure of observation [exists] across the country'. One might have imagined that intense observation would have provided opportunities for interactions with patients, but as Barre and Evans (2002) point out, the activity was often undertaken by healthcare assistants, often employed for the purpose on an *ad hoc* basis, and they quote Duffy (1995) that observation was often seen as 'a low status activity' that warranted delegation to assistants. This too was the position in this study. Without much doubt, such delegation reflected the custodial nature of the activity: yet again, the nursing staff were saddled with the task of ensuring that 'nothing happened on the ward'; observation seemed to be a precautionary mechanism, designed to avoid any untoward or problematic events that might disrupt the functioning of the ward and prevent its safe handover to the next shift. Typically, patients under observation were either suicidal or aggressive and what is remarkable is not the desire (understandable in these litigious times) to prevent a suicide or aggressive outbursts, but the manner by which intense or constant observation had acquired the low standing of a passive, even boring, undertaking. While Barre and Evans's (2002) discussion of the topic in terms of psychological defence mechanisms is recommended, we concluded that the determining factor mandating close observation was to ensure a 'safe ward'; an extension of the nursing responsibility for all aspects of patient's welfare even if, at times, this ran counter to what patients wanted. An interesting observation by Winbourne (2002) is that, as a patient in an acute ward, she believed that because her room was adjacent to a patient being observed she thought it was her being observed and not the other patient and she describes a quite hilarious sequence of events to which this misunderstanding gave rise.

We have already discussed the nature of evidence in *Chapter 2*, but it is pertinent to ask at this point, whose evidence determines practice? If the evidence of external agencies, such as the Department of Health and NHS Trusts, supports that notion of patients being contained—and custodialism appears to have re-emerged as an important psychiatric tool in recent year—what evidence can nurses assemble in support of therapeutic interventions and the playing down of the custodial role? The issue of closely observing individual patients could act as a catalyst for nurses to work out exactly why they still engage in their activities with such frequency: whose purposes are being served and how? In particular, does the nursing role extend into the moral responsibilities of patients such that nurses would substitute their responsibility for the patient's? What are the responsibilities of other disciplines and should that responsibility extend into participating in actual close observations? If nurses are to 'go it alone' on this issue, it would seem sensible that they work out a rationale for what they are doing. Of course, the problem is how to do this while operating within the straightjacket of psychiatric ward-based practice, its norms and obligations.

Gijbels and Burnard (1995) describe the nursing role as predominantly 'managing the environment and the patients, other nurses and themselves within it'. They portray the nursing role as 'keeping the place ticking over' by 'creating ward order, maintaining safety and ensuring patients got to where they were supposed to be on time'. Others have highlighted the nursing role as 'administration'; 'receiving, recording, organising and conveying information' and 'managing systems of care' (Cleary and Edwards, 1999; Machin and Stevenson, 1997; Whittington and McLaughlin, 2000).

Walton (2000) described how nurses focussed on ward management and not individual needs and how they strove to keep the ward mood stable, maintaining control of the environment from a distance and without necessarily becoming involved with individual patients. Pilgrim and Rogers (1994) coined the term 'benign non-interventions' to describe nursing activities that patients perceived as contributing to ward well-being; for example, making decisions about access to the ward kitchen, going on leave, TV scheduling, and so on.

The office

The focal point for much of this administration is the ward office and, in this study, an 'office culture' was observed on all of the wards. Qualified nurses were frequently observed trying to get out of the office, but they were often called back to deal with inquiries or phone calls: some of them stated that it was simply easier to 'stay put' and not venture out of the office at all.

Much of their office time was spent on retrieving and communicating information, an enterprise made difficult by the constantly changing staff complement across shifts. Despite lengthy periods spent in handover and frequent referrals to notes, much information seemed either to get lost or be held by only select members of the team. Nurses also played a key role in organising and facilitating multidisciplinary team meetings, as well as involving other professionals in patient care [thus fulfilling the 'intermediary role' defined for them by David Towell in 1975]. Much of their time was spent trying to track people down by phone or dealing with messages for other professionals visiting the ward. Nurses were instrumental in organising both admissions and discharges, both in terms of documenting and communicating the practical processes of this on behalf of almost everybody else. Indeed, our discoveries reflect a picture that has hardly changed in a generation. Consider Rosenhan's (1973: 255) description of a typical psychiatric ward at the time:

> 'Staff and patients are strictly segregated. The glassed quarters that contain the professional staff, which the pseudo-patients came to call the cage, sit out on every day room. The staff emerge primarily for care-taking purposes. Otherwise, staff keep to themselves, almost as if the disorder that effects their charges is catching.'

As the reference to pseudo-patients attests, Rosenhan's paper examined the deeper issue of how to differentiate between sane and insane: yet his descriptions of staff patient 'interactions' have a frighteningly recognisable quality about them.

Busyness

Throughout this study, the wards were busy more often than they were quiet. 'Busyness' was partly defined by:

a)   levels of activity (discharges, admissions, transfers, multidisciplinary meetings, ward visitors and routines);

b)   the acuity of the patient population (evidenced by disturbed behaviours, noise, patient numbers); and

c)   administrative and housekeeping demands and the constant ringing of the phone.

The busyness seemed to be a function not so much of these factors in themselves, but of the atmosphere that their multiple occurrence induced. An aura of 'busyness' stemmed more from staff's perceptions and expectations of what a ward ought to be rather than actual levels of activity or demand. Busyness, for example, invites the attention of managers by creating an image of a great deal being done at significant cost to those involved. For instance, the busyness would escalate rapidly whenever staff shortages occurred through sickness or if staff were engaged in off ward activities, such as escorting patients. Because of the feelings of stress and pressure induced by busyness, even when things quietened down some of the nurses were still unable to relax.

What nurses want to do

Various studies have noted how a lack of therapeutic interaction creates unease and discomfort for many nurses (Bowles, 2000; Bray, 1999; Cleary and Edwards, 1999). The conflicting demands to be therapeutic, while also fulfilling legal and other responsibilities, is cited as a main cause of distress (MacGabhann, 2000; Pilgrim and Rogers, 1994). Even when her interactions with staff had been largely negative, Rose (2000: 9) commented:

> *'I do not mean to imply that staff were nasty people, as individuals they were kind and personable. But in their role as nurses, they seemed to forget their communication abilities and turned into beings 'too busy' to extend the hand of help to people who really were in need of it.'*

Whittington and McLaughlin (2000) similarly attributed nurses' failure to function therapeutically to factors outside their control. For example, they witnessed nurses make arrangements to spend individual time with patients, with such good intentions being subsequently scuttled when administrative (often petty) demands intervened.

Many of the nurses interviewed here expressed disappointment that their expectations of psychiatric nursing contradicted the realities of inpatient settings: their conflicts lay between the desire to retain some idealism and the requirement to be pragmatic and 'make the wards run'. Some blamed their training for having created unrealistic expectations, and many challenged the value of academic ability when matched against practical skills. Some mentioned the futility of engaging therapeutically with patients if, at the end of the day, 'putting people through the system' was what mattered. These nurses believed that no one (for example, managers) paid attention to therapeutic work with patients as long as the latter came to no harm and were discharged in timely fashion. In interviews, nurses made clear their desire to work therapeutically with patients as well as indicating the sorts of patients they thought they should be working with. The rising numbers of personality disordered and addicted patients on the wards was an emotive issue and many described how this diverted them from working with 'madness' and forced them into nursing people with 'social problems'.

Staffing levels

Recommendation 7 of Acute Problems (Sainsbury, 1998) states, 'staffing levels and mix must be geared to the provision of effective care'. Other reports have highlighted how low staff levels, using bank and agency staff, and inadequate skill mix have negatively impacted on nurses responses to patients' needs (CRU, 2000; MacGabhann, 2000). Bowles (2000) argued that occupational dissatisfaction and stress resulted from an inability to focus on therapeutic activity and resulted in poor recruitment and retention of hospital nursing staff. Conversely, Whittington and McLaughlin (2000) found that, while increased numbers did result in more contact, it did not promote more interaction with patients. This is interesting and suggests that problems of interaction are rooted in beliefs about the nature of hospital nursing and are not simply a function of workload related to numbers.

Throughout, nurses repeatedly referred to inadequate staffing levels and poor skill mix, and the struggle to keep staff levels up was constant. Low staffing also had a significant impact on both short-term therapeutic activity and the ability to plan ahead and develop best practice and services. Inadequate staffing also contributed significantly to poor staff morale, both as a consequence of the immediate pressures created and also through the subsequent curtailment of time for supervision and training. At the same time, the fact of nurses, irrespective of their number, being rooted in archaic ward-based practices spoke volumes about how the customs and practices of organisations hold sway over individual's inclinations. In our view, the work patterns of the nurses were heavily constrained by the multiple pressures on them. However, when opportunities arose for doing individual therapy, these were not always taken advantage of. Somehow, the pressures exerted a sustained effect so that, even when the busyness subsided, the fallow period that followed seemed to represent a period of settling down before the next busy phase, a kind of 'calm before the storm'.

Environment

'Acute Problems' (Sainsbury, 1998) recommended that acute inpatient environments be designed to be both therapeutic and safe. However, problems exist when trying to reconcile goals, such as patient supervision and the need for privacy and personal space. Although we can be clear about what is not therapeutic, for example, cramped dirty conditions, drab decorations, tense atmospheres, etc., less consensus exists about what is therapeutic. For instance, opinions differ about the benefits afforded by single rooms as against the companionship of shared bed bays (Shields *et al*, 1988). Winbourne (2002), a service user, also believes that shared rather than single rooms are therapeutically beneficial. Achieving the balance between too little and too much space can be problematic (Bishop, 1979). The need for quiet areas has been cited by many as beneficial, but so also has the provision of social and recreational activities. Problems arise when different needs have to be met simultaneously and within the same confined space. Goodwin *et al* (1999) described ward environments as either tangible or non-tangible, the former being characterised by the physical environment and the space and resources contained within it, and the latter relating more to ambience and atmosphere. Godfrey and Wistow (1997) showed how non-tangible environments could vary enormously, despite the tangible environment remaining constant, and that finding was born out in this study where variations in atmosphere from positive to negative were not necessarily a function of physical surroundings; ie., we noted how the availability of suitable spaces in which to run groups or engage in one-to-one interactions did not affect the amount of therapeutic time spent with patients. Although quiet rooms were often available, these were most frequently used by other professionals or for administrative meetings.

Team dynamics and support for staff

'Addressing Acute Concerns' (SNMAC, 1999) predicted a continued downward spiral of inpatient settings, as poor working conditions meant greater difficulty attracting staff, thus perpetuating the negative experiences of existing staff. The inability of nurses to control their professional lives has been linked to increasing wastage, as well as being a poor incentive to others to replace them (Bowles, 2000). On a day-to-day basis, this is also evidenced in increasing amounts of sickness and absenteeism (Bray, 1999; Higgins *et al*, 1999).

Different reports have also identified a paucity of good clinical leadership as a major factor in low morale. 'Making a Difference' (Department of Health, 1999b) outlined a strategy for improving nurses' working lives, by promoting nursing influence over decision-making and strengthening clinical leadership. In the light of our findings, it is doubtful if these objectives have even begun to translate into action. Although we saw some examples of good leadership, in most areas, the lack of senior and experienced staff made excessive stress inevitable, particularly in newly qualified nurses who complained to us that their opinions were not sought nor, if offered, attended to.

Continual changes in service delivery are well documented in the literature and are reflected in the accounts of nurses in this project. For example, while the meaning behind organisational change seemed irrelevant to them, they nevertheless had to accommodate to its effects; ie., having to deal with a mixed patient population, the erosion of resources to meet the needs of these patients, and the insatiable demand on beds. For the nurses, there seemed to be a mismatch between service development and service need, and many stated that 'too much politics' undermined the real job of caring for patients. By 'too much politics' was meant too many mandates from central government added to which were local politics that comprised particular personalities and power balances.

Appropriateness

The problems of bed pressure have been variously attributed to an actual reduction in the numbers of beds, the rising morbidity of the population, a lack of community based resources, and increases in defensive practice (Bowles, 2000; Cleary and Edwards, 1999; MacGabhann, 2000). Mulholland (2000: 22) describes the problem succinctly:

'The ward is meant for 22, but there are easily twice that number; the professionals call it over occupancy; the patient's call it overwhelming. The doctors told one woman who came in suicidal that after two months she would be ready to leave. Three months later she is still there, waiting for the social worker to sort out her benefits before she can move to community provision. The professionals call this situation bed blocking. She simply finds it frustrating.'

There is some evidence that changing admission criteria, using short stay policies and other alternatives could improve the efficacy of bed usage (Bartlett *et al*, 1999; Johnstone and Zolese, 2002). Croudace *et al* (1998) suggest that increasing the number of beds is unlikely to provide a long-term solution (on the principle that increased provision increases need) and that more might be gained from looking at variances in practice around admission and discharge, the latter obviously linked to an enhanced community provision.

The inability to move patients on also caused frustration as well as perpetuating the pressure on beds. On all the wards, nurses identified patients who had been there for months and whose mental health was no longer a problem. One nurse described the wards as 'dumping grounds'. For us, the salient issue was the inability of the nurses to influence these factors other than by indirect, informal protest, protest that, ultimately, would be overruled by the medics when needed.

Course-based training

A fundamental problem to emerge in this study was the perceived dichotomy between practice requirements and basic (pre-registration) nurse education. These difficulties reflected the current debate concerning the relevant content and style of pre-registration courses (Faulkner, 1998; Gordon, 1998; Gournay *et al*, 1998; Hopton, 1997; Tarrier *et al*, 1999). Education that focussed on skills acquisition was valued and desired by some as was the role of 'learning on the job.' The nature of education and learning has explicit parallels with concepts of evidence described earlier. In this study, the type of learning seen as most useful was that linked to experience, learning from doing, and learning from others. Acquiring theoretical knowledge was appreciated, but only when it was directly related to experience or was illustrated in practice by senior colleagues.

It was clear that many of the nurses found difficulty in relating concepts to practice. This discrepancy reflects competing discourses about psychiatric nursing, and the compatibility of educational content to individual 'philosophies' of nursing. Gordon (1998) suggests that we should focus training on the development of critical appraisal skills and subsequent exploration of competing paradigms. This might be useful in the production of thoughtful nurses, but it does not reflect their expressed need for practical 'hands on' training.

Experiential learning

Kolb (1984) described learning as 'the process whereby knowledge is created through the transformation of experience'. According to Schon (1983), this is facilitated by processes of conscious and unconscious reflection on and within practice. Benner (1984) describes the clinical progression nurses make from over reliance on rules and guidelines to accurately appraising individual scenarios and responding intuitively as 'experts'. This process is supposedly facilitated by repeated exposure to practice experiences and an increasing ability to recognise patterns and connections between them. Similarly, nurses in this project described their learning as trying out approaches in different situations and developing confidence in their ability to select interventions and respond spontaneously.

Many nurses desired more contact with psychotic patients to 'normalise' their relations with them, so that their interactions would be less formulaic and based on more intimate understandings of their experiences. Nurses talked about learning from patients through listening to and observing their experiences of illness. Collaboratively working with patients was also described as promoting their own understanding and growth, a phenomenon previously described as central to therapeutic relationships (Peplau, 1952).

Learning from more experienced nurses occurred on several levels, but most nurses described the positive effects of being exposed to colleague's confidence—what one nurse called 'a net of confidence'.

Problems

There are problems with experiential and role model learning. Crook (2001) states that expert nurses are rarely aware of their 'expert status' or are unable to describe or quantify what makes them expert. Faulkner (1998) described a training programme based on junior colleagues 'picking up' experienced practitioner's skills. It proved unsuccessful and it was concluded that skills needed to be more clearly analysed and described in a language suitable to facilitate their dissemination.

The positive attributes of role models identified in this project were traits, such as calmness, thoughtfulness, and charisma. In addition, senior nurses who remained 'hands on' and 'focussed on patients' were seen to retain credibility and respect. What seems to be relevant here was less the provision of definitive characteristics that encapsulate expert nursing or good role modelling and more a recognition that combinations of factors, embodied as a cohesive and confident whole, appeared to work in defined contexts. Several nurses described how they selected different bits from different practitioners to inform their practice. Of course, the central flaw in imitative learning is an absence of critical review of that which is passed on, and this is just as likely to be bad practice as not.

Self-directed learning

Self-directed learning had a low impact on individual and team practice. Despite many of the nurses expressing an interest in research, they were often very vague about this and any familiarity with research appeared to be superficial. Parahoo (1999) found no differences in patterns of self-directed learning in more recently trained (Project 2000) nurses and those with an older style training, thus diminishing the widespread assumption that Project 2000 nurses would bring 'critical reflection' and 'research mindedness' into practice. We can corroborate Parahoo's findings: some nurses did attend workshops in their own time, but most were unwilling to allow encroachment on their personal time. Others who had completed courses were frustrated at their inability to integrate their newly acquired skills into practice and it is this last point that is central. For how can nurses devise even broad categories of practice on which they can agree when something as fundamental as the relationships between education and practice has yet to be worked out?

Interventions/approaches

The range of nursing interventions used with psychotic patients echoed competing discourses about both the nature of psychiatric nursing and the nature of evidence-based practice. A small minority subscribed to discrete frameworks, such as cognitive behaviour therapy, transactional analysis, or psychosocial interventions. However, the majority either identified more generic frameworks encompassing broad 'counselling' approaches, or intuitively grounded their approaches in experience. In general, broader approaches were seen as most useful. The only approach supported by all nurses was the use of medication.

Gournay *et al* (1998) describe initiatives, such as the Thorn programme and behavioural therapy training as 'substantial and significant advances in clinical skills.' These programmes allow nurses to practice in domains previously dominated by medics and psychologists. Accompanying these changes, 'basic' jobs previously done by nurses have been taken on by auxiliaries and other supportive staff. Tarrier *et al* (1999) viewed the adoption of psychological interventions by nurses, as 'very positive advances especially as these were being increasingly validated by research'. They considered that these innovations had not integrated into nursing practice because of the distance (literal and metaphorical) that lies between nurse education and practice. In inpatient settings, as we have seen, nurses have always resisted innovation and change. What seems required is an intensive input from educationalists and researchers working beside clinical teams, aimed at developing their skills through peer monitoring and support. Another important dilemma is that inpatient wards are frequently populated by patients with divergent mental health problems, a situation that promotes only one coherent approach, which is pharmacology. Nurses who were interviewed described the benefits of using psychological frameworks to address patient's problems. The question is whether it is possible to implement one 'all consuming' framework that relates to the broad range of patients that confront nurses in inpatient settings. Outside of a broad-based 'caring' approach, this seems unlikely, and frustrations (as well as benign custodialism) may continue for some time yet.

Influenced by a framework—general

In Hopton's (1997) view, the 1982 Mental Health Nursing Syllabus constituted a baseline of criticism of institutional and punitive nursing practice. In his view, the Syllabus led the profession into 'whole-heartedly embracing the theory and practice of humanistic/person-centred psychology and psychotherapy/counselling'. Hopton argued that:

'Mental health nurses' attachment to the theory and practice of counselling has now become so entrenched that if nurses, whether qualified or students, are asked to explain their clinical practice they almost invariably talk in terms of the theoretical and methodological imperatives of person-centred counselling, positive regard, empathy, active listening, and so on' (p496).

Bray (1999) confirmed this when his nurse sample described their role as 'being with patients, developing relationships, and generating trust.' MacGabhann (2000) found consensus among nurses and patients on the 'core elements of quality nursing,' namely 'spending time with patients, treating them with respect, enabling individual expression and caring'. These 'core' aspects were affirmed by many nurses in the present study, in opposition to those advocating more specific interventions, such as cognitive behavioural therapy. However, while the latter group figure significantly in academic nursing circles, among hospital nurses they are a small minority. Further, the nurses in this study were often unable to implement the broader-based caring approach they espoused because of the inhibitive (contextual) factors by which they were weighted down.

Medication

According to Bowles (2000), the resulting 'profound unease' of acute inpatient psychiatric nurses is leading to an increased use of medicating patients, as well as other defensive practices, such as seclusion. Peplau (1994) used to bemoan nurses spending their time administering medication and noted that: 'regrettably, some nurses report that giving pills to psychiatric patients has become the only treatment'. The picture is complicated and, although some nurses are hesitant about excessive use of drugs, few challenge their pivotal role. Using medication is dictated to an extent by the requirements of the Mental Health Act (Hopton, 1997; MacGabhann, 2000), and Working in Partnership (Department of Health, 1994) refers to the 'unique contribution of nurses in monitoring the dosage, effects and contra indications of medication'. This has to be balanced against the importance placed by others on humanistic aspects. In general, the place of medication and restraint was vouchsafed by most of our subjects and this may be seen as but the end point of a history of unswerving support, by psychiatric hospital nurses, for the use of psychiatric drugs.

Individual factors

For others, the core of nursing is 'understanding' patients, ie., understanding the 'truth' of their situation (Barker, 2000; Bowles, 2000; Goodwin *et al*, 1999). Barker's (2000) Tidal Model, for example, is daringly non interventionist in its aims:

'As nurses, in trying to be of help to the people in our care, we need to be careful that we do not devote all our energies to trying to control their experience of mental distress. We need to allow

people time to learn from reality so that they can become wiser about what has happened to them' (p60).

In *Chapter 2*, we concluded that 'evidence' offered for this kind of work is not going to satisfy conventional notions of what constitutes evidence. Tidal Model nurses would have to content themselves with definitions of evidence far removed from conventional beliefs about what evidence is: they would have to define their work in existentialist and person-centred terms. According to Loewenthal (1999: 250):

> *'It would appear that evidence must be based on research and that this research must be scientific, which means that it should be objective and this in turn ideally assumes a quantitative approach. Furthermore, anything worthwhile that is subjective is covered by qualitative approaches, which might be included if they can prove they are scientific'.*

However, Loewenthal points to a rich philosophical tradition that places subjective thought at the centre of human affairs. In a psychiatric context, this is hardly implausible and the notion of tapping into human experience as part of a research programme ought not to inhibit anyone. The preoccupation with evidence-based practice has highlighted aspects, such as 'randomisation' and 'results', and even if the political requirement may be to frame one's research as if it was scientific, it might be possible to present work based on the experiences of both users and professionals alike, and not to be unduly concerned about labelling it as 'evidence'.

In any event, consistent with other inquiries, we discovered practices that, at times, bordered on the anti-therapeutic; and even where nurses were attempting to implement one-to-one work with patients, this was curbed by the incessant demands of 'the ward', demands, which (often) had little to do with the direct care of patients. Perhaps what is needed is a hospital administrative class with responsibility for 'running the wards' so as to allow nurses to develop their therapeutic role. This would, of course, be expensive and is, in any event, improbable since much of what the nurses deal with might not be directly therapeutic, but nevertheless requires the kind of intimate knowledge of patients possessed by nurses.

What is needed, above all, is a recapturing of the spirit that the therapeutic community movement of the 1950s and 1960s represented. Therapeutic communities from this period (many of which continue to flourish) in their turn recaptured the spirit of the York Retreat, a Quaker run institution that tried to settle the minds of its inmates by dispensing kindness, warmth, civility, and open discussion. Contemporary therapeutic communities, although differing in important ways, start from the basic premises that their therapies have primacy of place. Their very existence depends upon underlying constructs of what therapy is and why it can help people. Unsurprisingly, some of these communities have had a tough time surviving in an evidence-based culture where evidence is construed in narrow outcome terms. While there were wards in the old psychiatric hospitals that adopted some of the therapeutic community principles, most backed off and continued along their primarily medical way. Adopting some of these principles would certainly help to unravel some of the archaic and moribund practices of inpatient wards. On the other hand, the operation of therapeutic communities usually requires a good degree of homogeneity among their patients, whereas acute wards exist for the sole purpose of accepting the widest array of disordered people consistent with the capacity of the nurses to 'manage' them. In order to make therapeutic communities work, therefore, it would be necessary to restructure wards so that their therapeutic functions would be clear and directed at defined groups of patients. The nursing teams would consist (partly) of named nurses whose sole responsibility would be to interact with patients across a whole range of fronts, but with the unified intention of promoting good mental health and recovery. Nurses would continue to liaise with other disciplines and perform functions, such as dealing with families and outside agencies, but only on the basis of doing good therapy. Under the present system, it becomes difficult to see how even modest proposals for change could be met.

Recommendations

The growing number of commentaries on the poor state of acute psychiatric, inpatient services, both in the nursing literature and in recent reports, is of major concern. At the same time, we have drawn attention to the positive practice that persists, despite the adverse circumstances that often militates against its taking place. We make especial effort to avoid any notion of attributing blame to actual nursing groups, preferring instead to perceive many of these problems as endemic to traditional hospital organisations and the manner by which nursing has come to be seen as a gofer profession, particularly in terms of the apparent willingness to service systems, which make possible the ongoing dominance of medical psychiatry and its need to ape medical organisation via the retention of ward-based beds.

We acknowledge the growing body of relevant and evidence-based interventions that could be integrated and developed in acute inpatient nursing, but we believe that there needs to be minimum practice standards established across services before this can be considered. Allowing that this investigation revealed levels of practice which, at times, barely rose above chaotic, attempts to inculcate practice that is evidence-based seem premature, and probably unworkable given the oppressive conditions in which practice is delivered. It is, in fact, the nature of how and why hospitals systems are organised as they are that requires attention. The provision of evidence that this or that intervention works is of little use when implementing interventions is persistently hamstrung by the 'ward's needs'. The current potential and natural resources that exist in the nursing workforce do need to be recognised and exploited. There are strong expectations of improvements in practice from patients, carers, service managers, and central government that are all important, and successfully accommodating them merits urgent consideration. But, to begin with, the fundamental structure and purpose of actual wards needs to be examined and perhaps questioned. These wards service a medical perspective on mental illness and its treatment. Essentially, this perspective is predicated on the notion of signs and symptoms not as subjective phenomena requiring to be addressed in an interactive way, but simply as objective manifestations of illnesses for which the primary treatments are physical. Under such a perspective, the acute ward as a 'holding pen' makes some sense: the patients are contained by the nurses, for whatever duration is required for them, to be treated by the medical team. Historically, the majority of psychiatric nurses have appeared, implicitly at least, to support such systems, although as others and the authors of this book have found, not without some misgivings. Nurses of all kinds are nowadays set on examining their role in respect of their occupational status in relation to other disciplines. Additionally, they are being called on by others to account for their role in respect of working with patients. There appears to be a consensus that their performance cannot be legitimised via their connection with the medical profession. It remains unclear to what extent these preoccupations are the preserve of some nurses with the majority continuing to support the status quo. Assuming that there is a groundswell of positive opinion for change, we believe that the only viable way forward is for inpatient nurses to challenge the very nature of what they have been doing: to look towards creating something new rather than merely patching up what they have already got.

The recommendations listed here have major implications for further exploration, investment, and development of services at organisational, educational, and ward levels. The scale of what is required is potentially overwhelming, so much so that ward-based nurses might, understandably, feel damned by an inability to change anything. These problems have been aired so often, however, that any continued avoidance of tackling them could be seen as straightforward obtuseness.

Recommendation One

Services need to re-establish the content and primacy of fundamental nursing and identify minimum standards relating to practice in these areas.

Recommendation Two

Services and education should develop more ward-based learning opportunities through the provision of training with good practice by expert practitioners on the wards.

Recommendation Three

Services should create posts dedicated to practice and education development and to facilitate the implementation of recommendations one and two.

Recommendation Four

There needs to be a review of the criteria for the admission and subsequent management of people described as having borderline personality disorders. An attempt should be made to reach local consensus on guidelines and policy relating to people with these disorders. Their separate management from other groups of patients needs to be considered.

Recommendation Five

A consultation process should be initiated to explore perceptions of the role of the inpatient setting with patients and carers. This should involve community staff, service managers, educationalists and ward-based nurses, so as to facilitate the development of more realistic and consensual expectations.

Recommendation Six

Extending recommendation five, consideration needs to be given to the abolition of acute inpatient psychiatric wards as they are currently structured. Their continued existence fly in the face of any evidence that supports their efficacy, other than as holding bays where patients are 'managed' during the time they are awaiting or undergoing medical intervention. Lumping different diagnostic categories together is detrimental to care, and other, community-based, alternatives need to be explored. In particular, grouping patients with similar problems would allow nurses to develop appropriate skills. It would also enhance the meaningfulness of the patient's experience of inpatient care.

References

Aggleton WB, Chalmers H (1986) Nursing research, nursing theory and the nursing process. *J Adv Nurs* **11**(2): 197–202

Altschul A (1997) A personal view of psychiatric nursing. In: Tilley S, ed. *The Mental Health Nurse*. Blackwell Science, Oxford: 1–4

Altschul A (1972). *Patient-Nurse Interaction. A Study of Interaction Patterns in Acute Psychiatric Wards*. Churchill Livingstone, London

Antoniou J (2000) Back in one piece. *Nurs Times* **96**(40): 23–24

Baker S (2000) *Environmentally Friendly*. MIND Publications, London

Bannister D (1998) The nonsense of effectiveness. *Changes* **16**(3): 218–20

Barker P (2000) The tidal model of mental health care: personal caring within the chaos paradigm. *Ment Health Learn Disabil Care* **4**(2): 59–63

Barker P, Cutcliffe J (1999) Clinical risk: a need for engagement not observation. *Ment Health Pract* **2**(8): 8–12

Barre T, Evans R (2002) Nursing observations in the acute inpatient setting: a contribution to the debate. *Ment Health Practice* **5**(10): 10–14

Bartlett C, Holloway J, Evans M, Harrison G (1999) Projection of alternatives to acute psychiatric beds: review of an emerging service assessment method. *J Ment Health* **8**(6): 555–68

Becker HS, Geer BG (1960) Participant observation: the analysis of qualitative field data. In: Adams R, Oreiss J, eds. *Human Organisation Research*. Dorrey Press, Illinois: 267–89

Benner P (1984) *From Novice to Expert*. Addison-Wesley Publishing, New York

Bishop J (1979) The environment of the therapeutic community. In: Hinshelwood R, Manning N, eds. *Therapeutic Communities— Reflections and Progress*. Routledge and Kegan Paul, London: 59–67

Bowles A (2000) Therapeutic nursing care in acute psychiatric wards: engagement over control. *J Psychiatr Ment Health Nurs* **7**(2): 179–84

Bracken P, Thomas P (1999) Campaigning against coercion. *Openmind* **96**, March/April, 7

Bradshaw A (2001) *The Project 2000 Nurse: The Remaking of British General Nursing 1978-2000.* Whurr, London

Bray J (1999) An ethnographic study of psychiatric nursing. *J Psychiatr Ment Health Nurs* **6**(4): 297–305

Briggs A (1972) *Report of the Committee on Nursing. Cmnd: 5115,* HMSO, London

Bruyn ST (1970) The methodology of participant observation. In: Filstead WJ, ed. *Qualitative Methodology: Firsthand Involvement with the Social Order.* Markham Publishing Company, Chicago: 305–27

Buckeldee J, McMahon R (1994) *The Research Experience in Nursing.* Chapman and Hall, London

Burns N, Grove SK (2001) *The Practice of Nursing Research: Conduct, Critique and Utilisation,* 4th edn. WB Saunders, London

Butler RA (1974) *Interim Report of the Committee on Mentally Abnormal Offenders. Cmnd.* Home Office and DHSS, London

Caudill W (1958) *The Psychiatric Hospital as a Small Society.* Harvard University Press, Cambridge, Mass

Chambers M (1998) Interpersonal mental health nursing: research issues and challenges. *J Psychiatr Ment Health Nurs* **5**(3): 203–11

Chenitz WC (1986) Getting started: the research proposal for a grounded theory study. In: Chenitz WC, Swanson JM, eds. *From Practice to Grounded Theory.* Addison-Wesley, Reading, Mass: 39–47

Clarke L (1996) Participant observation in a secure unit: care, conflict and control. *Nurs Times Res* **1**(6): 431–40

Cleary M, Edwards C (1999) 'Something always comes up': nurse-patient interaction in an acute psychiatric setting. *J Psychiatr Ment Health Nurs* **6**(6): 469–77

Cobb AK, Hagemaster JN (1987). Ten criteria for evaluating qualitative research proposals. *J Nurs Educ* **26**(4): 138–43

References

Cohen L, Manion L, Morrison K (2000) *Research Methods in Education*, 5th edn. Routledge, London

Coleman R (1999) *Recovery: An Alien Concept?* Handsell, Gloucester

Cook TD, Campbell DT (1979) *Quasi Experimental Designs and Analysis Issues for Research.* Rand MacNally, Chicago

Cormack D (1991) *The Research Process in Nursing.* Blackwell Scientific Publications, Oxford

Cormack D (1976). *Psychiatric Nursing Observed.* RCN, London

Crick M (1976) *Explorations in Language and Meaning: Towards a Semantic Anthropology.* Malaby Press, London

Crook J (2001) How do expert mental health nurses make on the spot clinical decisions? A review of the literature. *J Psychiatr Ment Health Nurs* 8(1): 1–5

Croudace J, Beck A, Singh S, Harrison G (1998). Profiling activity in acute psychiatric services. *J Ment Health* 7(1): 49–57

CRU College Research Unit (2000) *National Audit of the Management of Violence in Mental Health Settings.* Final Year Report. Royal College of Psychiatrists, London

Cullum N (1997) Identification and analysis of randomised controlled trials in nursing: a preliminary study. *Q Health Care* 6(1): 2–6

Cutcliffe J (1997) The nature of expert psychiatric nursing practice: a grounded theory study. *J Clin Nurs* 6(4): 325–32

Davis BD (1981) Social skills in nursing. In: Argyle M, ed. *Social Skills and Health.* Methuen, London: 31–54

Dennis S (1997) Conflict in Care? *Ment Health Nurs* 17(5): 5–6

Department of Health (1999a) *The National Service Framework for Mental Health Service.* HMSO, London

Department of Health (1999b) *Making a Difference.* HMSO, London

Department of Health (1998) *Modernising Mental Health Services. Safe Sound and Supportive.* HMSO, London

Department of Health (1997) *The New NHS.* HMSO, London

Department of Health (1994) *Working in Partnership.* HMSO, London

Duffy D (1995) Out of the shadows: a study of the special observations of suicidal psychiatric inpatients. *J Adv Nurs* **21**(5): 944–80

ENB (2000) *Teamworking in Mental Health: Zones of Comfort and Challenge.* ENB Research Highlights, London

Etzioni A (1960) Interpersonal and structural factors in the study of mental hospitals. *Psychiatry* **23**: 13–22

Faulkner J (1998) A head start. *Nurs Times* **94**(43): 39

Field PA, Morse J (1985) *Nursing Research: The Application of Qualitative Approaches.* Croom Helm, London

Ford R (2002) Opinion. *Ment Health Pract* **5**(9): 26

Foucault M (1977) *Discipline and Punish: The Birth of the Prison.* Allen Lane, London

Gamble C (1995) The Thorn Nurse Training Initiative. *Nurs Stand* **9**(15): 31–34

Germain CP (2001) Ethnography: the method. In: Munhall PL, ed. *Nursing Research: A Qualitative Perspective*, 3rd edn. Jones and Bartlett Publishers, London: 277–306

Gijbels H, Burnard P (1995). *Exploring the Skills of Mental Health Nurses. Developments in Nursing and Health Care 5.* Avebury, Aldershot

Glaser BG, Strauss AL (1967) *The Discovery of Grounded Theory: Strategies for Qualitative Research.* Aldine, Chicago

Godfrey M, Wistow G (1997) The user perspective on managing for health outcomes: the case of mental health. *Health Soc Care Commun* **5**(5): 325–32

Goding L, Edwards K (2002) Evidence-based practice. *Nurse Researcher* **9**(4): 45–56

Goodwin L, Holmes G, Newnes C, Walthon D (1999) A qualitative analysis of the views of in-patient mental health service users. *J Ment Health* **8**(1): 43–54

Gordon N (1998) Influencing mental health nursing practice through the teaching of research and theory: a personal critical review. *J Psychiatr Ment Health Nurs* **5**(2): 119–28

Gouldner AW (1971) *The Coming Crisis of Western Sociology.* Heinemann Educational, London

References

Gournay K (1996) Schizophrenia: a review of the contemporary literature and implications for mental health nursing, theory, practice and education. *J Psychiatr Ment Health Nurs* **3**(1): 7–12

Gournay K, Birley J, Bennett D (1998) Therapeutic Interventions and milieu in psychiatry in the NHS between 1948 and 1998. *J Ment Health* **7**(3): 261–72

Herbert M (1990) *Planning a Research Project: A Guide for Practitioners and Trainees in the Helping Professions*. Cassell, London

Higgins R, Hurst K, Wistow G (1999) *Psychiatric Nursing Revisited. The Care Provided for Acute Psychiatric Patients*. Whurr Publishers, London

Hopton J (1997) Towards a critical theory of mental health nursing. *J Adv Nurs* **25**(3): 492–500

Hudson L (1966) *Contrary Imaginations*. Penguin Books, Harmondsworth

Humphreys J (1996) English nurse education and the reform of the health service. *J Educ Policy* **11**(6): 655–59

Illingworth P (1999) Return to sender. *Nurs Times* **59**(38): 27–28

Jehu D (1972) Research methods. Unpublished Paper, School of Social Work, University of Leicester, Leicester

Johnstone P, Zolese G (2002) Length of hospitalisation for people with severe mental illness. (Cochrane Review) In: *The Cochrane Library*, Iss 2. Update Software, Oxford

Jolly K, Bradley F, Sharp S, Smith H, Mann D (1998) Follow-up care in general practice of patients with myocardial infarction or angina pectoris: initial results of the SHIP trial. *Fam Pract* **15**: 548–55

Jones J, Lowe T, Ward M (2000) Inpatients' experiences of nursing observation on an acute psychiatric unit: a pilot study. *Ment Health Learn Disabil Care* **4**(4): 125–29

Kierkegaard S (1941) *Concluding Unscientific Postscript*. Princeton University Press, Princeton

Kikuchi JF, Simmons H, Romyn D (1996) *Truth in Nursing Inquiry*. Sage, London

Kitson A (1997) Using evidence to demonstrate the value of nursing. *Nurs Stand* **11**(28): 34–9

Kitson A, Ahmed LB, Harvey G, Seers K, Thompson D (1996) From research to practice: one organisational model for promoting research-based practice. *J Adv Nurs* **23**(3): 430–40

Kolb D (1984) *Experiential Learning: Experience as the Source of Learning and Development.* Prentice-Hall, London

Laing RD (1960) *The Divided Self.* Tavistock, London

Laing RD, Esterson A (1964) *Sanity, Madness and the Family,* Vol 1. Penguin Books, Harmondsworth

Leff J, Kuipers L, Berkowitz T (1982) A controlled trial of social intervention in the families of schizophrenic patients. *Br J Psychiatry* **141**: 121–34

Lepola I, Vanhanen L (1997) The patients' daily activities in acute psychiatric care. *J Psychiatr Ment Health Nurs* **4**(1): 29–36

Loewenthal D (1999) Editorial: what is evidence and what is research? *Eur J Psychother Couns Health* **2**(1): 248–50

Lofland J (1976) *Doing Social Life: The Qualitative Study of Human Interaction in Natural Settings.* John Wiley & Sons, New York

Lofland J, Lofland LH (1984) *Analysing Social Settings: A Guide to Qualitative Observation and Analysis,* 2nd edn. Wadsworth Publishing, CA

Ludemann R (1979) The paradoxical nature of nursing research. *Image* **11**(1): 2–8

MacGabhann L (2000) Are nurses responding to the needs of patients in acute adult mental health care? *Ment Health Learn Disabil Care* **4**(3): 85–88

Machin T, Stevenson C (1997) Towards a framework for clarifying psychiatric nursing roles. *J Psychiatr Ment Health Nurs* **4**(2): 81–87

Mair M (1998) Letter to editor. *Changes* **16**(3): 220

Martin JP (1984) *Hospitals in Trouble.* Blackwell Science, Oxford

May D, Kelly MP (1982) Chancers, pests and poor wee souls: problems of legitimation of psychiatric nursing. *Sociol Health Illness* **4**: 279–301

Medawar P (1972) *The Hope of Progress.* Methuen, London

References

Melia K M (1982) 'Tell it as it is'—qualitative methodology and nursing research, understanding the student nurse's world. *J Adv Nurs* **7**(4): 327–35

Menzies I (1960) *Social Systems as a Defence Against Anxiety*. Tavistock, London

Menzies Lyth I (1988) *Containing Anxiety in Institutions*. Free Association Books, London

Midgley M (2001) *Science and Poetry*. Routledge, London

Miller WL, Crabtree BF (2000) Clinical research. In: Denzin NK, Lincoln YS, eds. *Handbook of Qualitative Research*, 2nd edn. Sage Publications, London: 607–31

Mischler E (1979) Meaning in context: is there any other kind? *Harvard Ed Rev* **49**: 1–19

Moore C (1998) Acute in-patient care could do better, says survey. *Nurs Times* **94**(3): 54–56

Moore LW, Miller M (1999) Initiating research with doubly vulnerable populations. *J Adv Nurs* **30**(5): 1034–40

Morrall P (1998) *Mental Health Nursing and Social Control*. Whurr Publishers, London

Morrison P (1991) *Caring and Communicating: The Interpersonal Relationship in Nursing*. Macmillan Education, Basingstoke

Mulholland H (2000) We just can't go on like this. *Nurs Times* **96**(40): 22

Parahoo K (1999) Research utilisation and attitudes towards research among psychiatric nurses in Northern Ireland. *J Psychiatr Ment Health Nurs* **6**(2): 125–35

Peplau H (1994) Psychiatric mental health nursing: challenge and change. *J Psychiatr Ment Health Nurs* **1**(1): 3–7

Peplau H (1952) *Interpersonal Relations in Nursing*. Putnam, New York

Perkins R (2000) Solid evidence? *Open Mind* **101**, January/February: 6

Pilgrim D, Rogers A (1994) Service users' views of psychiatric nurses. *Br J Nurs* **3**(1): 16–18

Polit DF, Hungler BP (1993) *Nursing Research—Methods, Appraisal and Utilisation*, 3rd edn. J B Lippincott Company, Philadelphia

Popkewitz TS (1984) *Paradigm and Ideology in Educational Research: The Social Functions of the Intellectual.* The Falmer Press, London

Popper K (1959) *The Logic of Scientific Discovery.* Hutchinson, London

Porter S (2000) Qualitative research. In: Cormack D, ed. *The Research Process in Nursing*, 4th edn. Blackwell Science, Oxford: 141–51

Porter S (1991) Qualitative analysis. In: Cormack D, ed. *The Research Process in Nursing*, 3rd edn. Blackwell Science, Oxford: 330–40

Quint JC (1967) The case for theories generated from empirical data. *Nurs Res* **16**: 109–14

Radcliffe M (2002) United in opposition. *Nurs Times* **98**(29): 22–24

Ragucci A (1972) The ethnographic approach to nursing research. *Nurs Res* **21**: 485–90

Richardson R, Droogan J (1999) Implementing evidence-based practice. *Prof Nurse* **15**(2): 101–4

Ritter S (1997) Taking stock of psychiatric nursing. In: Tilley S, ed. *The Mental Health Nurse: Views of Practice and Education.* Blackwell Science, Oxford: 94–117

Robertson MHB, Boyle JS (1984) Ethnography: contributions to nursing research. *J Adv Nurs* **9**(1): 43–9

Rolfe G (2000) *Research, Truth and Authority: Post-modern Perspectives on Nursing.* Macmillan, Basingstoke

Rose D (2000) A year of care. *Open Mind* **106**, November/December: 8–9

Rosenhan D (1973) On being sane in insane places. *Science* **179**: 250–58

Sainsbury (1998) *Acute Problems: A Survey of the Quality of Care in Acute Psychiatric Wards.* Sainsbury Centre for Mental Health, London

Sapsford R, Abbott P (1992) *Research Methods for Nurses and the Caring Professions.* Open University Press, Buckingham

References

Schatzman L, Strauss A (1973) *Field Research.* Prentice-Hall, New Jersey

Schon D (1983) *The Reflective Practitioner: How Professionals Think in Action.* Temple Smith, London

Schwartz MS, Schwartz CG (1955) Problems in participant observation. *Am J Sociol* **60**(4): 343–53

SEC (1999) *Sussex Educational Consortium.* Falmer, Brighton

Sharp V (1975) *Social Control in the Therapeutic Community.* Saxon Books, Lexington, Mass

Shepherd G, Murray A, Muijen M (1994) *Relative Values: Different Views of Users, Family Carers and Professionals on Services for People with Schizophrenia in the Community.* Sainsbury Centre for Mental Health, London

Shields PJ, Morrison P, Hart D (1988) Consumer satisfaction on a psychiatric ward. *J Adv Nurs* **13**(3): 396–400

Shotter K (1975) *Images of Man in Psychological Research.* Methuen, London

Silverman D (1989) The impossible dreams of reformism and romanticism. In: Gubrium JF, Silverman D, eds. *The Politics of Field Research: Sociology Beyond Enlightenment.* Sage, Beverley Hills, CA: 30–48

Simpson A (1998) *Creating Alliances.* Sussex Education Consortium

SNAMC (1999) *Standing Nursing and Midwifery Advisory Committee. Mental Health Nursing: Addressing Acute Concerns.* HMSO, London

Stern PN (1980) Grounded theory methodology: its uses and processes. *Image* **12**(1): 20–3

Stevens R (1976) *Integration and the Concept of Self.* The Open University Press, Milton Keynes

Stuart GW (2001) Evidenced-based psychiatric nursing practice: rhetoric or reality? *J Am Psychiatr Ass* **7**(4): 103–11

Sullivan P (1998) Developing evidence based care in mental health nursing. *Nurs Stand* **12**(31): 35–38

Szasz T (1974) *The Myth of Mental Illness.* Harper and Row, New York

Tarrier N, Barrowclough C, Haddock G, McGovern J (1999) The dissemination of innovative cognitive-behavioural psychosocial treatments for schizophrenia. *J Ment Health* **8**(6): 569–82

Tordoff C (1998) From research to practice: a review of the literature. *Nurs Stand* **12**(25): 34–37

Towell D (1975) *Understanding Psychiatric Nursing*. RCN Publications, London

Walton P (2000) Psychiatric hospital care—a case of the more things change, the more they remain the same. *J Ment Health* **9**(1): 77–88

West WG (1980) Access to adolescent deviants. In: Shaffir WB, Stebbins RA, Turowetz A, eds. *Fieldwork Experience: Qualitative Approaches to Social Research*. St Martin's Press, New York

White R (1985) Political issues in British nursing. In: White R, ed. *Political Issues in Nursing*, Vol 1. John Wiley, Chichester: 19–43

Whittington D, McLaughlin C (2000). Finding time for patients: an exploration of nurses' time allocation in an acute psychiatric setting. *J Psychiatr Ment Health Nurs* **7**(3): 259–68

Wiles R (1998) Patients' perceptions of their heart attack and recovery: the influence of epidemiological evidence and personal experience. *Soc Sci Med* **46**: 1477–86

Wilson HS, Kneisl CR (1988) *Psychiatric Nursing*. Addison-Wesley, New York

Winbourne R (2002) Personal communication

Wittgenstein L (1968) *Philosophical Investigations*, 3rd edn. Blackwell Scientific, Oxford

Index